THE PHYSICISTS

C.P. SNOW
THE PHYSICISTS

Introduction by William Cooper

M

TO MY NIECE, STEFANIE

First published 1981
by Macmillan London Limited
London and Basingstoke

Associated companies in Auckland, Dallas,
Dublin, Hong Kong, Johannesburg, Lagos, Manzini,
Melbourne, Nairobi, New York, Singapore, Tokyo,
Washington and Zaria.

Designed and produced for Macmillan London Ltd by
Bellew & Higton
Bellew & Higton Publishers Ltd
19–21 Conway Street London W1P 6JD

Computerset by MFK Graphic Systems (Typesetting) Ltd,
Saffron Walden, Essex

Printed in Great Britain by Morrison & Gibb Limited

ISBN 0 333 32228 2

Contents

M ost of us can remember the first time we heard or read something which seemed to throw a new light upon the world. In my own case, it comes back with extreme clarity. I was a child of eight or nine, and I had got hold of a bound volume of Arthur Mee's *Children's Encyclopaedia*. It was a dark afternoon, and I was sitting by the fire. Suddenly, for the first time, I ran across an account of how atoms were supposed to be built up. The article had been written before Rutherford had discovered the nucleus, although by the time I read it the nuclear atom must have been well known. However, I was innocent of all that, I had never seen the word 'atom' before; this article – it was quite short and was contained, I think, in a section called the Child's Book of Wonder – explained that its descriptions were only a guess, that no man knew the truth, and yet it seemed to open up a new sight of the world.

It told me that if you could go on cutting up any sort of material, you would arrive at atoms in the end. These atoms were so small that no one would ever see them and you could crowd countless millions on to a pin point. There were different sorts of atoms: and yet, if you cut up the atoms themselves, you found in some mysterious way that they were made of the same stuff. That idea probably came more easily to a child than to an adult, and I swallowed it whole.

The actual description of these atoms was rather quaint, in the light of later knowledge. Small as they were, they were packed with much smaller things called electrons (which, of course, had been known about since J. J. Thomson's work in the nineties). According to the article, these electrons were like tennis balls in a cathedral; and, again according to the article, the tennis balls were in violent and random motion across the interior of the cathedral. It is a little difficult nowadays to see how that picture was ever conceived; I found it very easy to unlearn a few years later.

Yet, though so much of that article could not endure, it gave me the first sharp mental excitement I ever had. Somehow it gave me the heightened sense of thinking and imagining at the same time. And one is lucky if those exalted moments visit one more than ten or twenty times in a whole life. . . .

From 'The first excitement that knowledge gives': editorial by the author in *Discovery*, April 1939

Introduction

The Physicists is a first draft, completed just before his death on 1 July 1980, of a book which C. P. Snow intended to write at greater length – he planned in particular to put more material in the last chapters. However, written as it was, straight off and at great speed, it has an unimpeded narrative impulse together with a completeness over the period of time, which simply ask for it to stand on its own as a literary work.

When he first told me about the book, I said: 'Good God, you'll have to do some research for that, won't you?' To which he replied: 'I'm writing it largely from memory.' I was silenced. He had one of the most remarkable memories I'd ever come across, a constant source of envy to me. Furthermore, we'd been close friends for nearly fifty years – in fact ever since the time when I was a Cambridge undergraduate reading physics, sent to him, then a Research Fellow of the College, to be taught – and so I was qualified to understand that he didn't always do exactly what he said he was doing, not absolutely exactly. Wrong again! When I read the draft I recognized that it actually had been written largely from his memory. It's odd – memory, even a memory as comprehensive as his, has its selectiveness, its patches, its things that stand out for reasons of other than factual importance. When an artist calls upon memory, what he writes has a life and a moving quality which scarcely ever infuses the product of the filing cabinet which we nowadays refer to as researched information.

A la recherche du temps perdu the book naturally took me straight back, at the beginning, to the days in the early 1930s when I myself was going to lectures by Rutherford and Dirac and Kapitsa, days so glorious that even my memory recalls something of their heroes. Rutherford, big and fresh-complexioned, his spectacles shielding light, transparent eyes, was indeed boomingly Jehovianic, albeit in an attractive way – one could see how the physicists near to him came to give him such devotion. Looking back on it, one is tempted to speculate on how far the aggressive boom, like Anthony Trollope's aggressive boom, had grown as an outer protective shell –

Snow remarks on this in the book – for a more sensitive, delicately responding nature. (Actually Blackett, in later years, always struck me as more Jehovianic – tall, thin, high-shouldered, with wavy hair and a flashing eye, in manner altogether loftier, nobler, graver: more of a Jehovah's Jehovah, perhaps.)

Dirac was very, very different – taciturn in both languages, as Snow remarks. Quantum mechanics, whether one could understand it or not, was clearly the creation of a remarkable mind; but at five o'clock of a winter's evening in an over-heated lecture-room, one would have given anything for the exposition of a remarkable mind's creation to be illumined by just the occasional human spark of temperament. Kapitsa, on the other hand, provided a running succession of human sparks of temperament, a lot of them of a wonderfully clowning kind, typically Russian, and typically deceptive – struggling with the English language, he appeared to keep getting things wrong and having to put them right. His broad face was smiling, his hair sticking straight out from its parting, and his nose, blunt and fleshy, making one wonder if that was the sort of nose Dostoievsky described as 'plum-shaped'. Everyone loved going to Kapitsa's lectures.

But I'm writing about Snow and his *Weltanschauung*, not embarking on a supplement of my own to *The Physicists*. (I'm tempted to make a quip to the effect that his *Weltanschauung* – a good word from the 1930s – seemed to me as comprehensive as his memory, with insights penetrating the worlds of science, of literature, of human affairs.) I'd recently been reading through some of the public speeches he made throughout the latter half of his life, about science and scientists, human affairs and human beings: reading through *The Physicists* I was frequently reminded of them; a sentence in the book setting up a resonance – one of his favourite words – with the beginning of a train of thought that he had followed at length, elsewhere on some other occasion, to a revealing conclusion.

A first case in point – his reference in the book to Arthur Schuster's deliberate resignation from the Chair of Physics at Manchester University, in order to make way for Rutherford, resonated with his account of an incident three hundred years ago, when the Cambridge Professor of Mathematics, named Barrow, resigned his Chair on condition that his pupil was appointed to it, his pupil being Isaac Newton – an account with which Snow began his 1962 Rectorial Address to the University of St Andrews, 'On magnanimity'. The essence of the address was a plea for magnanimity in our use of scientific and technical knowledge for 'seeing to it that the poor of the world don't stay poor. . . .'

> The great majority of the world's population don't get enough to eat: and from the time they are born, their chances of life are less than half of ours. These are crude words: but we are talking about crude things, toil, hunger, death. For most of our brother men, *this* is the social condition. It is different from *our* social condition. That is one reason why there is a direct call upon our magnanimity. If we do not show it now, then both our hopes and souls have shrivelled. It may be a longish time before men at large are much concerned with hopes and souls again.

I have quoted the passage because to my mind it illustrates Snow's realistic view – some people, myself included, would call it a dark view – of human nature, counterbalanced as it was in his own nature by another strong element, that of hope; and a belief that our hope's coming to fruition depends on men's magnanimity. He was one of the most magnanimous of men, in all senses, public and private, I've ever known. I venture to suggest that the dark view, the hope, and the magnanimity all shine through *The Physicists*.

And, by God, when he comes in his story to The Bomb, the hope and the magnanimity are more than necessary. (The dark view comes, as it were, in the package.) Incidentally, it's fascinating to note, *à propos* his remarking in the book that the scientific facts essential to making the bomb were commonly known among scientists *before* the war, the publication in *Discovery* (a scientific journal Snow edited) of a notice in April 1939 of Hahn's discovery in Berlin of uranium-splitting, and in May 1939 of Joliot's discovery in Paris of what were subsequently called chain-reaction neutrons. Snow himself in the May 1939 issue wrote an editorial, 'Science and air-warfare', in which he attempted to reduce the then current hysteria about the excessively destructive effects of air-attack with TNT bombs – about which, as those were the attacks we subsequently survived, he turned out to be correct. But in September 1939 his editorial was entitled 'A new means of destruction'. The world had changed. (Just to put things into perspective, it's also fascinating to recall that in 1913 H. G. Wells, in *The World Set Free*, had forecast something like an atomic bomb.)

The world had changed, and after 1945 it was riven by the moral issue arising in the first instance from the destruction of Hiroshima and Nagasaki. There may have been some justification for Hiroshima: for Nagasaki I, like many of the physicists, believe there was none. If ever the dark view of human nature had a profound source, the destruction of Nagasaki touched that source. The book tells the story of how the physicists understood and responded to the moral situation they were in, tells it movingly and magnanimously. The issue in a broader sense has since become, and remains today, one of such emotional, intellectual and moral significance to everybody, scientists and non-scientists alike, that I am including at the end of his book a speech in full, called 'The moral un-neutrality of science', which Snow delivered to the American Association for the Advancement of Science in 1960. Snow's view of science as an intrinsically moral activity (in the sense that it is an undeterred search for observable truth), which has a moral influence on the men and women who engage in it, is a view which we talked about and which meant a great deal to him. It strengthened his belief that it was through science and technology that we could, and must, 'see to it that the poor of the world don't stay poor.'

Yet 'The moral un-neutrality of science' doesn't say the last word about the dilemmas in which physicists, and scientists in general, found themselves after the war. Up till 1945 dilemmas were well below the surface: the Hitler war, as Snow calls it, had to be won. And for that purpose the bomb had to be made and secrecy had to be kept, and there was no difficulty about it. In those days Snow and I were hiving off selected physicists into what was artfully called the Directorate of Tube Alloys, of whose function I had only the vaguest intimations to begin with. Then, along with the intimations taking clearer, fearful shape, there was a half-saving grace which I always remember being expressed by F. Simon, another distinguished Jewish refugee physicist, holding a Chair at the Clarendon Laboratory in Oxford: a dark, starless night, and Simon walking with us to the gateway of the Clarendon – we had been working late – and he said: 'I *hope* it won't work. . . .' Spoken with great prescience and deep emotion; yet I felt sure that *au fond* he knew it actually was going to work.

It did work, and after 1945 the physicists were burdened with the moral dilemma over the making and the using of the bomb; and on top of that the dilemma over secrecy – which in effect meant keeping things from the Russians. That latter dilemma sharpened as the Cold War came into being, sharpened as the conflict between loyalty to the nation-state and loyalty to the individual conscience became absolutely explicit. That dilemma, too, may be one to which there is no solution in the abstract; and

Snow himself seems to recognize that. In 'The moral un-neutrality' his view appears to go one way: in another speech, called 'State v. individual' it appears, if not to go the other way, at least to be unresolved.

> Human affairs, it seems to me, depend upon a degree of trust. If, within one's own society and state, one can't rely on that degree of trust, the social life becomes, to put it mildly, precarious. Individual conscience is essential and mustn't be denied. But often it isn't a sure guide to action. As a general rule, it isn't a guide sure enough to let one break one's obligations and one's oaths. That, for me at least, is a general rule. Clearly there are situations when it wouldn't be over-riding. The problem is, as in all ethical problems in real life as opposed to the textbooks, where the line is drawn.

Nevertheless, although during the Hitler war secrecy obtruded in the lives of professional scientists who until then, especially during the Golden Age, had never given a thought to it; although it has still not been cast out – as well as national secrecy we now have commercial secrecy, God wot – Snow still considered the scientific profession to be the one that offers its members the greatest *freedom*. (He did not die – as Wells did, seeing many of the things he'd hoped for not having come to pass – in despair, far from it.) In 1970 he delivered a speech at Loyola University in Chicago, 'Freedom and the scientific profession', in which realistic acquiescence to the way the world was going is uplifted by hope. As I have used the word 'freedom' myself, I must quote his menacing opening paragraph about it.

> Freedom is a word that needs using carefully. Too often we have used it as a political slogan and done ourselves no good in the process. If you use words for political purposes, they soon lose whatever meaning they may have had. If you are tempted to brandish the word 'free', remember that over the gates of Auschwitz there stretched – and still stretches – the inscription *Arbeit Macht Frei*. Language is the most human thing about us: in a sense, the invention of language made us human: but language, perhaps for the same reason, is the greatest expression of human falsity, or if you like, of original sin.

So much for the word 'free'. Snow excludes both the political and metaphysical usages, and concentrates on its usage in our day-to-day living, particularly in our working-lives.

> It was in order to avoid that kind of subjectivity that I chose some questions which we can all answer. They are matter-of-fact questions, just as the freedom to which they refer is a matter-of-fact freedom. I don't apologize for this. Unless we know what being free means in our working-lives, we aren't

likely to be specially sensible about what being free means anywhere else. Well then. How free are you to choose your work? From day to day? From year to year? How free are you to explain it? To say what you think about it? How free are you to earn your living through your work? In your own country? In other countries? Anywhere in the world?

And then in answer:

Of all the people I've known, the only group who would say 'Yes' to that whole set of questions are the professional scientists. Even then not without qualification and distinctions, which I shall come to presently. But, by and large, professional scientists have the possibility of acting more freely than any other collection of human beings on earth. Answering my simple questions, they can say – at least as soon as they are out of their apprenticeship or training for research – that they can choose what kind of work to do. Their subject for research – that is at their own disposal, just as much as what a writer selects to write about or a painter to paint. Very few of us have that degree of freedom: certainly no politician has, though the more inflated may fool themselves that they have. And the scientists are entirely free to publish what they have done, how and where they please: they are under no constraints: they can publish the results of their work however they like. Unlike other kinds of creative person, they are normally not interested in any kind of commercial influence. There is another fact which separates them decisively from the rest of us. Their skill is international in the fullest sense. No other group of professional people (except perhaps musicians and ballet dancers) can say as much. A scientist has the potential to earn his living, and to do his proper work, anywhere. Many have demonstrated this.

The qualifications have to be taken seriously. Especially in the physical branch of the scientific profession, for those physicists who have remained or become soldiers-not-in-uniform: they are restricted in their choice of work, in their movement from country to country, and in their right to publish. The next restriction upon physicists comes with the necessity, as Snow remarks in the book, to work, if they want to choose particle-physics, in teams and wherever the necessary large machines happen to be. The third comes from safety: that is a restriction that is looming ever more ominously over the work of molecular biologists, and genetic engineers.

Yet, realistically acquiescing to the increasing articulation of society and conceding the restraints that arise therefrom, Snow still sees the scientific profession as the one to which the replies to his questions come nearest to a universal 'Yes' – a 'Yes' that is strengthened by the increasing importance of science in the post-industrial society, by the expansion of its scope and the funds devoted to it. And even in an era when nationalism is having a grisly recrudescence everywhere, science remains above all *international*. The great majority of scientists have a wider choice than the rest of us, in our professions, of what topic they'll work on: they are freer than the rest of us to move to any country where that work is going on; and when they publish the results of their work, it can be, and it is, read all over the world. From this Snow in the speech draws his conclusion:

> I have been speaking, deliberately, about one of the most privileged groups of human beings – in my view the most privileged group bar none in the world today. I have no doubt that they will continue to be as privileged, relative to the rest of us. So that they set a kind of limit when we think of what we others can realistically expect of free behaviour in an increasingly interlinked society. That is why I have talked so practically and prosaically. Free behaviour, being free, acting freely in our existential choices, freedom – they are not usually helpful concepts in our life as we live it. What we need, I think, especially when we are young, is a sense of non-utopian expectations: of measuring our expectations against what people are doing in their professional existence. The professional existence I have selected is the one which most clearly points towards the future. In some ways, as I have said, its members will by the end of the century not have the option to behave as freely as they do now. In some ways they have increased degrees of freedom. There is nothing to be pessimistic about. If our expectations are anywhere near right, the scientific profession will still provide a desirable life, within the human limits. If we hold up that model as something which other working-lives can aspire to, we still won't do badly. It is a better model than other ages have had: much better than that of the Homeric warriors or the Norman pattern of chivalry or the philosophers of the Early Church: much better, and believe it or not, much more genuinely free.

William Cooper
LONDON, DECEMBER 1980

1
The direction of time's arrow

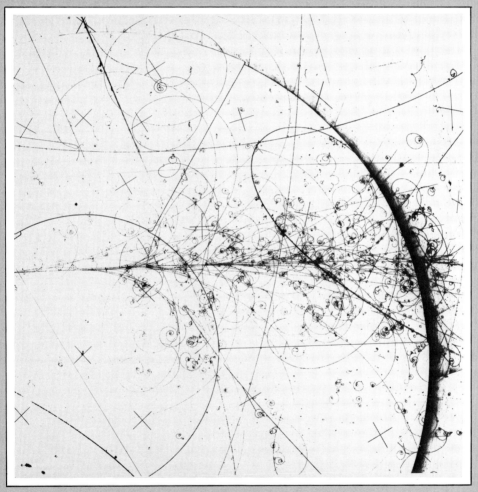

Bubble chamber picture of a neutrino interaction. Neutrinos are
fundamental particles which have no charge and no mass. Predicted by
Fermi in the 1930s, they were first discovered in the 1950s

In not much over a generation, physicists have changed our world. That applies to the most elemental of situations, life and death. Nuclear weapons are an achievement of applied physics. To many people they have brought a new kind of fear. It is hard to be cool-headed about this, in the atmosphere of our times. Perhaps a look at the present situation of the world, including the state of modern physics, will help us to see things with calmer eyes. Even so, it isn't comfortable to live with the thought that it is within human power to exterminate a sizeable fraction of the world population within a matter of hours.

It won't do any harm, however, to be reminded that applied physics can have an entirely benevolent face. The most dramatic example, as will be seen when this account comes to an end in the year 1980, may be the prospect of abundant energy for ever. If this happens, it will be when nuclear fusion (a process which produces the energy of the hydrogen bomb) is controlled for peaceful purposes. If this happens, and it is not a certainty, then we shall have a new source of social hope. It is the most exciting promise that applied science has yet suggested – not a firm promise so far, but more than a dream.

The gifts of applied science – and this will have to be said more than once – are two-faced. We have to see that the benevolent face gets the better of it. That is, of course, the public responsibility of all of us. It is going to need tough and farsighted minds, not easily paralysed by dread. The possibility of nuclear energy is a good example in front of us here and now.

These results – there are plenty more – come through the physicists' power over the natural world. This has happened very quickly, and has become concrete in the space of a generation. The roots of these changes go back further, to the emergence of nuclear and electronic physics, but even that is not very far away, almost within an old man's lifetime. This book will attempt to tell about some of the people who played a part – to begin with, naturally enough, without any clear idea of where their thoughts and actions were leading. It is a mistake to imagine that the founding fathers of modern physics were actively concerned with practical applications. With almost all of them, that was a subsidiary interest, if as much as that.

That certainly wasn't the motive which drove them on. The essential motive, if one is going to simplify, was curiosity. The old name for their subject was natural philosophy, as it still is in Scottish universities, and that gives a better impression of what they were trying to do. They wanted to understand the natural world. Anyone who can add even a little to such understanding, as Einstein said, has been granted a great grace. Understanding the natural world was enough to engross any man's power, and enough to justify any man's life.

For a good many of the personages in this account – including those who were serious world citizens and more reflective than most of us – the first time that they were meshed into immediate practical problems was in the Second World War, and then out of bitter necessity. They proved to be singularly effective; Fermi is a star example. A number remained influential in applied science afterwards, but many longed for the peaceful days of the 1920s, which still glow as the golden age of natural philosophy. Mark Oliphant, more eloquent and outgoing than most, spoke for them just after the war: 'We couldn't have done anything else, but we have killed a beautiful subject.'

Oliphant was and is a strong man, but that was a *cri de coeur*. (Later in his life he became Governor of South Australia; almost the only scientist of high achievement to occupy such a position.) However, events have proved that he underestimated both the dynamic of natural philosophy and the shortness of human memory. True, physicists have never quite recaptured the hopeful and benevolent internationalism of the 1920s, when their community was the nearest approach our century will know to an 'island of peace'. Still, the great edifice of physical science has continued to be built, one of the few human activities where only a fool could deny the reality of progress. There is no progress in art, just change. Today's writers write differently from Homer and Aeschylus, but they don't write better.

Our understanding of the natural world shows, like nothing else in human enterprise, the direction of time's arrow. Isaac Newton was, by common consent, the greatest scientist who has ever lived: but any adequate A-level student now knows more about the physical universe than Newton could have done. Incidentally, the recent additions to the edifice of physics have not only revealed more of the details of the physical universe; they have shown the universe to be a far stranger place than we could have conceived even thirty years ago. We have learned to accept notions such as antimatter, black holes in space, and the bewildering properties of quarks – the ultimate constituents of matter. Scientific discovery is a process without limits, as Newton realized three hundred years ago, when he said, 'I seem to have been only like a boy playing on the seashore, and diverting myself in now and then finding a smoother pebble or a prettier shell than ordinary, while the great ocean of truth lay all undiscovered before me.'

2
From macrocosm to microcosm

Faraday's laboratory at the Royal Institution

Michael Faraday, professor of chemistry at the Royal Institution. He was
the greatest of the experimental physicists. Portrait by Thomas Phillips, c. 1842

Whehn did modern physics begin? That isn't a question with much meaning, since the process is continuous. For our present purposes, we can make a crude statement about physicists, practically and intellectually. Modern physics began with the discovery of the particles of which atoms are made: first electrons, then protons and neutrons. These discoveries began to be made in the last years of the nineteenth century.

Through most of the nineteenth century, classical physics was advancing fast. Scientists were studying the large-scale laws of matter and energy: Newton's law of gravitation explained how the planets and stars move; the laws of thermodynamics laid bare the properties of energy and heat, with practical results in the steam engine; and electricity and magnetism were being swiftly unravelled. Some people, even eminent scientists, believed that scientific effort was getting near to its end, and that there remained only mopping up operations – they sensed the day of total victory in man's understanding of the physical universe. The same feeling, that scientists have reached final statements, has occurred in other domains of science since: it has always been an intuition gone wrong. They were not greatly concerned with the structure of matter on the smallest scale. The general run of scientists assumed that matter was made of atoms, indestructible, eternal, and that these presumably differed from one element to another, as chemical experiments indicated.

Chemists, far more than physicists, were concerned with atoms, for it was now clear that chemical reactions were simply the rearrangement of atoms into larger groupings called molecules. Chemists knew the relative weights of the atoms of the different elements. The Russian chemist Mendeleev had found that when he arranged the elements according to their atomic weight, curious patterns emerged – elements with similar chemical properties recurred at regular intervals. Although physicists thought vaguely there must be something in Mendeleev's law, they usually brushed the topic aside. Atoms were a convenient concept – especially for chemists – but the major nineteenth-century physicists had plenty to keep them busy without speculating about atoms.

The physicists were settling the great laws, the macrocosmic laws, of electromagnetism and thermodynamics, as difficult to penetrate as the microcosmic laws of their successors, and obviously of immense applied significance. Faraday was the greatest of experimental physicists (the only competitor being Rutherford in the next century) and he applied his gifts to probing the properties of electricity and magnetism, and the relation between them. When Faraday started his researches, electricity and magnetism were nothing but playthings. Before he died, the laws of the electromagnetic field were being worked out, and big electrical industries were already set up, though not in his own country.

Faraday was one of the saints of science, gentle, unassuming, generous, preserving the virtues of the Sandemanian sect (a relaxed derivative of Calvinism) in which he was brought up. He was one of the very few of the great scientists to be born among the very poor. Somehow he was spotted as a bright and dexterous lad, and he became a laboratory assistant to Sir Humphry Davy, who treated him with some condescension (as from parvenu bourgeois to proletarian) but gave him a kind of scientific opening. Faraday didn't repine. Quite rapidly, he became one of the Victorian glories, and his lectures at the Royal Institution one of London's treats. Dickens offered to help write the lectures so as to make them accessible to a wider audience. Victorians were remarkably good at recognizing and celebrating their own great men.

Meanwhile another man of supreme gifts was at work turning Faraday's results into mathematical form – one of the great theoretical feats of the nineteenth century. Clerk Maxwell was, like Faraday, a man of unusual sweetness and light. Unlike Faraday, he was comfortably off, a Scottish landowner, and when his health failed (he died in his forties) he retired from the Cavendish Chair of Physics to his own estate. The Chair had just been created at Cambridge, thus initiating the only research school in England at a time when American universities such as Michigan had already had well-organized research for thirty years past. Maxwell left a pleasant legend in Cambridge. He was high spirited and entertaining. His only vice was the writing of indifferent light verse with an obsessive facetiousness that has since been emulated by other scientists.

There was another mind, at least as powerful as Maxwell's, operating

James Clerk Maxwell, first professor of experimental physics at
Cambridge

in hermit solitude on the other side of the Atlantic. Willard Gibbs was,
single-handed, establishing the conceptual laws of thermodynamics, and
thus the whole of classical physical chemistry. Originally, thermodynamics was the science of how heat and energy are related, and the impetus of
studying it came from the practical importance of the steam engine.
Gibbs's theoretical insight discovered that the same laws of thermodynamics control the chemical reactions between atoms. It was said
that you had only to read Gibbs's great works to understand everything
about chemical thermodynamics – but since his exposition was in a
notation known only to himself, it would probably be easier to work the
subject out for oneself. Gibbs was a shy eccentric, something like Kant,

with habits so regular that people could set their watches by him. He lived with his sister in New Haven, and was impossible to stir. He was, along with the analytical philosopher C. S. Pierce, the most original abstract thinker born in America so far. It is uncommon to meet an American student who has heard either of those two great names.

Theirs were the heights of classical physics before the modern age (more correctly the particle age) began. Of course, classical physics didn't end in the 1890s, when the electron was discovered. Essential work is being done today. Most of the problems of hydrodynamics and aero-dynamics are solved by applying the laws of classical physics. G. I. Taylor, one of this country's most gifted theoreticians, devoted his life to them, except when he was called on like a fire-engine for one of the jobs that required his superlative technical mastery – as when he computed the properties of the blast-wave from a nuclear explosion. The principles of space travel are classical, and Tsiolkovsky, the early twentieth-century Russian scientist-engineer of genius who predicted much of what has occurred, would have no difficulty in making his way round a modern space centre were he still alive – he would no doubt wish that he could have laid his hands on our metallurgy and propellants.

Pierre and Marie Curie in 1896. Together they investigated radioactivity, first at the Paris School of Physics and Chemistry, then at the Sorbonne

Still, classical physics lost its dominance and there was a change of direction among physicists, somewhere near the turn of the century. The initiative didn't come from abstract thought, but from some puzzling observations (much more as romantics expect scientific revolutions to start, though history often tells us otherwise). With the development of efficient air pumps, scientists could now investigate air – and other gases – at very low pressures. When an electric current was passed through such a gas, physicists were surprised to find 'rays' streaming off one of the electrodes (the cathode). A German physicist, Eugen Goldstein, christened them cathode rays – but what were they?

In 1895, another German physicist, Wilhelm Roentgen, found that cathode rays produce another, even stranger, type of radiation when they hit a solid object. He called them X-rays: X for unknown, for these highly penetrating rays were unlike anything then known. The following year, a French physicist, Henri Becquerel, found that minerals containing uranium also produce radiation, quite spontaneously. Where did radiation come from? Clearly from components of the mineral itself – but how? It is not known whether any of the early observers guessed that the answer was individual atoms. Scientific papers are always written as though no one ever anticipated anything.

Much of this activity was taking place in Paris. That itself was rather odd, for France at the time wasn't as scientifically developed as England or Germany. Academic salaries were meagre, and laboratory equipment primitive beyond belief. (The latest TV film of Marie Curie and her husband Pierre at work in Paris minimizes, rather than exaggerates, the paucity of resources with which they had to do their work.) But people with the scientific obsession aren't easily put off by poverty of that kind. Rutherford used to boom: 'I could do research at the North Pole.'

There was a lot of determination and ability in Paris: in addition to Becquerel there was the Polish woman, Marie Sklodovska, who had just become Madame Curie, and the young Paul Langevin who was eventually to invent – among other things – sonar. In a partly accidental, but scientifically meticulous, fashion, some of the first discoveries in modern physics were made. The Curies isolated a new element, and called it radium. Radium had various curious properties; for example, it had a finite lifespan, losing weight by degrees as it emitted several distinct kinds of radiation. The idea that atoms might not always be permanent, but could sometimes disintegrate of their own accord, hung vaguely in the air.

Then J. J. Thomson proved in 1897 that cathode 'rays' were not waves of radiation at all – Thomson deflected them with both magnetic and electric fields, evidence that they were minute particles of matter each carrying an electric charge. His experiment also showed that these particles – electrons – weighed far less than hydrogen atoms. That is, particles of a different order from any atoms were proved to exist. It took some years for scientists to guess or realize that these particles could be emitted from atoms themselves, or to speculate that atoms were not simple but had constituents of their own. From the first, these results cut across the grain of most preconceptions. There were classical physicists who died unconvinced. But in fact this convulsion of scientific thought, like those which came later, was quickly domesticated. Scientific reason showed itself too strong for doubt.

The existence of the electron was soon taken for granted. As a matter of history, there was something of a personal row. Who had really discovered the electron? Who had the priority? Scientists, as a great practitioner, Peter Medawar, has recently reminded us, are very much like other people. They come in all shapes, sizes, temperaments. Some are very clever, as the outside world judges cleverness. Some aren't. Some are noble, and again, some aren't. There are often disputes about priority, and they can be very bitter. Newton, it is sad to say, was venomously ungenerous in this respect. Charles Darwin was magnanimous, and so was Alfred Wallace, who arrived at Darwin's conclusions about the evolution of the species at the same time.

That may have happened over the electron. Philipp Lenard, a German physicist, certainly thought so, and said so with vehemence. He also said, with even more vehemence, that he had got in first. But he didn't get the major credit, which went to the Cavendish Professor, J. J. Thomson. Most neutral opinion seems to have thought that there was no injustice done. As someone said, in a great discovery the scientist must satisfy two criteria. He must know what the discovery is, and he must know how important it is. Thomson satisfied both criteria. He had a much more lucid intellect than Lenard who, incidentally, as an old man was one of the only two eminent German scientists who became active spokesmen for the Nazi faith. (The other was Werner Heisenberg, a great theoretician not yet born at the time of Lenard's dispute with Thomson.)

When the electron had been identified, there was no doubt from that time on about the existence of sub-atomic particles. Electrons must be an

The Curies in their laboratory. In 1903 they shared the Nobel prize for physics with Henri Bequerel for their discovery of polonium and radium, elements which disintegrate spontaneously with the emission of alpha particles

Sir Joseph John Thomson, Cavendish professor of
experimental physics from 1884 to 1918

integral part of every atom, and Thomson replaced the earlier, chemists' concept of the atom as a structureless 'billiard ball' with a more sophisticated model. Thomson's atom was a diffuse sphere of positive electric charge, with the negatively charged electrons embedded in it. In the cathode ray tube electrical forces ripped the electrons out of the residual gas atoms and sent them flying down the tube as 'cathode rays'.

At last physicists began to take the atom seriously, and began to think about its interior structure. Many of the best minds in physics became devoted to the structure of microcosmic matter. Within forty years they had consummate success.

Overleaf: The makers of the new atomic physics at the second Solvay Conference in 1913

VERSCHAFFELT   LAUE RUBENS GOLDSCHMIDT
HASENOHRL   JEANS   BRAGG   M⁽ᶜ⁾CURIE SOMME

NERNST   RUTHERFORD   WIEN   J.J.THOMSON WARBURG

LINDEMANN DE BROGLIE POPE GRUNEISEN   HOSTELET
TEIN   KNUDSEN   LANGEVIN

BRILLOUIN BARLOW KAMERLINGH-ONNES WOOD GOUY WEISS

3
Founding fathers

Ernest Rutherford, professor of experimental physics and
director of the Cavendish Laboratory, Cambridge, from
1919 to 1937. Chalk drawing by F. Dodd, 1934

The Cavendish Laboratory's million-volt generator for
accelerating charged particles, 1937

Those forty years, that is from the end of the nineteenth century to the outbreak of the Second World War, were a wonderful time for physicists to be alive. Both experimental physicists and theoreticians had their phases of triumph, and it is instructive to notice how the balance swung. There was a long record of experimental discoveries beginning with elucidation of the radiations emitted from radioactive elements and evidence that most of an atom's mass lay in a central nucleus. Rutherford and Chadwick's disintegration of atoms by particles from radioactive sources led on to disintegration of atoms by controlled means by Cockcroft and Walton. Meanwhile there was identification of further sub-atomic particles – neutrons and positive electrons. And in 1938 the most fateful experiment of all, the splitting of some uranium atoms with an emission of particles which could lead to further splitting, with the possibility of a chain reaction and the release of huge amounts of energy.

Through most of this period, the dominant figure was Ernest Rutherford who was born in 1871. As has been said, he ranks with Faraday among British experimental physicists. As a man, he was wildly different from Faraday – exuberant, outgoing, not noticeably modest or unassuming. He was taken at face value, a simple face value, by most of the people round him. Internally, he was not so simple. There were deep layers of diffidence concealed beneath that robust and noisy façade. He was a prey to nerves. He found it hard to manage an overweighted nature. Kapitsa, one of the most gifted of his pupils, an engineering-physicist of genius in the high Russian tradition, and in addition equipped with psychological observation and insight, seems to have been the only member of Rutherford's scientific entourage who understood him well. Kapitsa's letters to his mother in Leningrad, dating from the time he first came to England to work with Rutherford, have recently been published in the Soviet Union. Within a few days Kapitsa was writing, 'The Professor is a deceptive

Peter Kapitsa at the opening of the Ludwig Mond
Laboratory, Cambridge, in 1933

character. They [the English] think he is a hearty colonial. Not so. He is a
man of immense *temperament*. He is given to uncontrollable excitement. His
moods fluctuate violently. It will need great vigilance if I am going to
obtain, and keep, his high opinion.'

About the only item true in the stereotype of Rutherford is that he was a
colonial. His father was a Scottish immigrant to New Zealand, who
managed after scraping a living, doing odd jobs, to become a small farmer
and a kind of general utility man, employing one or two workmen and
doing anything in the way of domestic repairs. He seems to have had a
good deal of technical ingenuity.

Rutherford knew nothing in the way of privilege. New Zealand was a
remote province. He received a good education, however, rather on the
Scottish model. He was top of his school in all subjects, being very far from
the dumb-ox kind of scientist who occasionally turns up. But when he
came to England on a scholarship he felt an outsider who didn't know the

rules. There were a good many chips on those heavy shoulders. He couldn't get along with English intellectual chit-chat, and insisted on behaving like a country boy who had never read a book (actually he was very widely read) with people of about one-hundredth of his cultivation, not to say intelligence.

He was a great man, and a good one. He didn't like being outfaced, though, by people who had learned tricks denied him. He wasn't comfortable in the company of well-trained theoreticians. Of course he could have mastered theoretical physics, or anything else in science, but some of those shoulder chips got in the way. When he was Cavendish professor, Cambridge became the world centre of experimental physics, but it didn't rank with Copenhagen and Göttingen in theory – except for the accidental occurrence of a young theoretical physicist of great genius, Paul Dirac. His appearance had nothing to do with Rutherford; that the divide in Cambridge between theoretical and experimental physics was sharp, did have something to do with Rutherford.

As a physicist, he had extraordinary intuition. He seems scarcely ever to have tried a problem which wouldn't go. If any scientist had a nose for, to use Medawar's phrase, 'the solution of the possible', Rutherford had. His attack was simple and direct, or rather he saw his way, through the hedges of complication, to a method which was the simplest and most direct.

An example is the most dramatic event of his career, the experiments by which he proved the existence of the atomic nucleus. The Curies had shown that radium emits various kinds of 'radiation', and one of these was now known to consist of a stream of electrically charged particles. These 'alpha particles' were identical to helium atoms with their electrons removed; but they originated not from helium gas but sprang spontaneously from the radium atoms as they disintegrated.

Even though atomic disintegration was still little understood, Rutherford saw these high-speed alpha particles as useful projectiles. He intercepted them with a thin sheet of gold foil, to see what happened as they passed through. If atoms were diffuse spheres of electrical charge, as Thomson had imagined, then most of the alpha particles should have gone straight through; a few should be deflected slightly. But some of the alpha particles bounced straight back again. It was like firing artillery shells at a piece of tissue paper, and getting some of them returning in the direction of the gun.

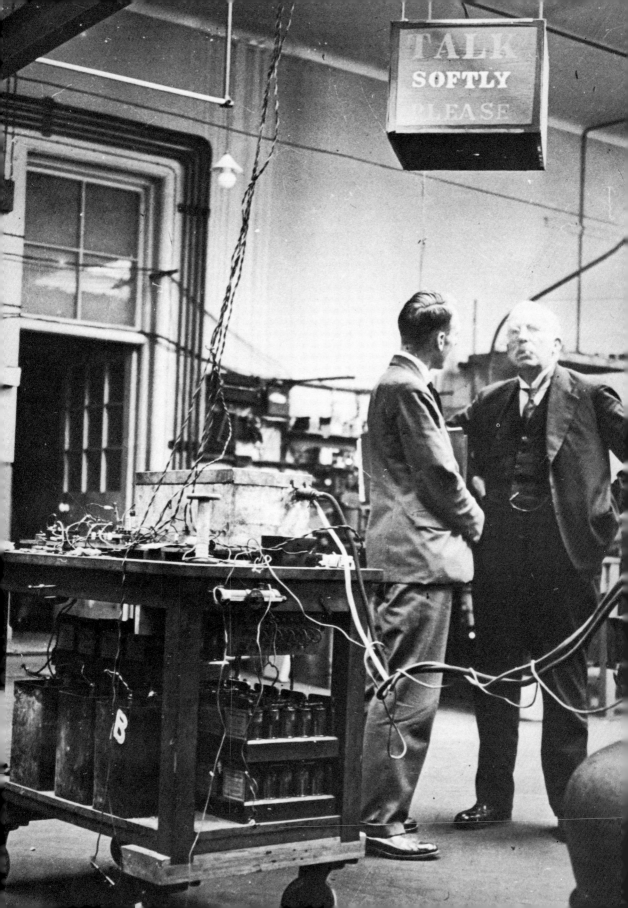

Rutherford could only explain this by postulating that these alpha particles were hitting small, massive concentrations within the atoms. He thus concluded that most of an atom's mass resided in a minute, positively charged nucleus at the centre, while the electrons went around the outside – very much like the planets orbiting the massive sun. Most of the atom was just empty space. If an atom were expanded to the size of the dome of St Paul's Cathedral, virtually all its mass would lie within a central nucleus no larger than an orange. The large majority of alpha particles passed the atoms' emptiness and carried on through the foil; but just occasionally one would hit a nucleus head-on, and rebound along the way it had come.

Positive, like all Rutherford's physics. He said that he knew it was convincing, and maintained that he was completely surprised. One wonders if he hadn't had a secret inkling. He was superlatively good at making predictions about nature.

It is hard to think of a prediction of his which didn't come off. He predicted the existence of an electrically neutral particle within the atomic nucleus, which was duly proved when Chadwick discovered the neutron in 1932. He predicted the splitting of atoms by accelerated protons, duly achieved by Cockcroft that same year. He made just one negative prediction: as late as 1933, he announced that the energies in the atom were unlikely ever to be used. That apart, he was almost always right. His Cavendish 'boys' as he called them – men as gifted as Chadwick, Kapitsa, Cockcroft, Blackett (all Nobel prize winners), Oliphant, Dee, half a dozen others – tended to think that, though he might be overpowering or deafeningly noisy, he was next door to infallible.

That was his kind of paternal leadership. His own greatest individual work wasn't done at Cambridge at all. With singular folly, Cambridge didn't try to keep the young Rutherford – possibly because the place wasn't big enough to hold both him and his seniors. He went off to a professorship at Montreal. American universities bid for him, better talent-spotters than Cambridge, but at the time America wasn't a major force in the scientific world, and Rutherford returned to England, after a touching and deliberate resignation by the head of the physics department at Manchester, Arthur Schuster, who thought that Rutherford must at any cost be preserved for this country. It was at Manchester that Rutherford proved the nuclear structure of the atom.

Rutherford (right) and J. Ratcliffe at the Cavendish. The 'Talk softly please' notice was aimed at Rutherford whose booming voice upset the apparatus

Overleaf: Physics research students at Cambridge in 1933. The crocodile on the wall of the Mond was the work of Kapitsa, a joking reference to Rutherford

W.J.Henderson. W.E.Duncanso

C.B.O.Mohr. N.Feather. C.W.Gilbert. D.Shoenberg.

B.B.Kinsey. F.W.Nicoll. G.Occhialini. E.C.Allberry. B.M.Crowthe

J.K.Roberts. P.Harteck. R.C.Evans. E.C.Childs. R.A.Smith. G.T.P.Taff

Miss.Sparshott. J.A.Ratcliffe. G.Stead. J.Chadwick. G.F.C.Searle. Prof.Sir.J.J.Thomso

...ght. G.E.Pringle. H.Miller.

...a. R.Witty. — Halliday. H.S.W.Massey. E.S.Shire.

...den. W.B.Lewis. P.C.Ho. E.T.S.Walton. P.W.Burbidge. F.Bitter.

...ray. J.P.Gott. M.L.Oliphant. P.I.Dee. J.L.Pawsey. C.E.Wynn-Williams.

...Lord Rutherford. Prof.C.T.R.Wilson. C.D.Ellis. Prof.Kapitza. P.M.S.Blackett. Miss.Davies.

It is instructive to remember how little money was spent on these great scientific researches. Faraday's apparatus (some still preserved in the Royal Institution) was humble, knocked up in the laboratory. Things hadn't changed much by Rutherford's time. His experiments were built with the help of one laboratory technician, or if he were feeling well-financed, perhaps two. There was no engineering. All was home made. The old phrase was 'string and sealing wax', and it is not far from the truth. The Cavendish was a great experimental laboratory, but it would look like a badly equipped high school compared with the big physics institutions of today. It was not until trained engineers such as Kapitsa and Cockcroft became active that the Cavendish knew any approach to big physics. Rutherford marvelled and cheered them on, but sometimes thought that it might be overdone.

Until the Second World War, there was little industrial support for physicists. Chemists had been looked after by the chemical industry for many years: other industries had been peculiarly obtuse in not seeing any conceivable use for physicists. Young men in the 1930s, with doctorates and good research to their credit, considered themselves lucky to get decent jobs in schools. A few years later, in the war, they were being snatched up as the rarest and most valuable of all human commodities.

It seems strange now that the Cavendish at its peak should have stayed so remote from industry. With the harsh wind of approaching war, however, Cockcroft, the Cavendish all-purpose functionary, was set to indoctrinate selected young men in the latest military prospect – what was later called by the American name of radar, and was the most successful British scientific weapon in the Hitler war. Few unobtrusive steps have paid off better. By the by, that happened in the same university which contemporary opinion seems to believe was devoted entirely to espionage.

Rutherford and his colleagues had little to do with money. It seems to have bored Rutherford himself about as much as academic philosophy. He was a remarkably unmercenary man. He could have earned large fees as a consultant. He would have thought that a ludicrous waste of time. As a professor at Montreal he was paid £500 a year. At Manchester and Cambridge he got about £1600, a good academic salary for the period, but he never earned more than that. When he died, he left almost exactly the amount of his Nobel prize, which at that time was something like £7,000.

In that brilliant period, an even rarer character was leaving his mark on world physics. This was Albert Einstein. He was born in 1879, and thus was eight years younger than Rutherford. When he was in his twenties, people were talking of him as the new Copernicus. A little later, it wasn't unusual or extravagant to say that here, for the first and only time, was someone in the class of Newton.

Einstein's greatest work touched only remotely on the new particle physics. His Theory of Relativity – actually in two parts, Special Relativity and General Relativity – made him rightly world-famous. But it dealt not with the small-scale structure of matter, but the largest scales of space,

Albert Einstein in the 1920s. Before he was forty he was the world's most celebrated scientist

time and speed. Ironically enough, relativity was at the time so controversial that Einstein was not awarded his Nobel prize for the greatest of his theories, but for some early work on the effect of light on metal surfaces. His explanation of this photo-electric effect, however, did form an important basis on which later particle physicists could build when they came to describe atoms in terms of quantum theory – of which more later.

Einstein was the most independent of all great scientists, relying with absolute confidence on his own solitary thoughts. He had set out to understand all aspects of the natural world: space, time, the unity and harmony of the entire world picture. He had set out to find the most universal of universal laws. He did so.

Ink and pencil caricature of Einstein by
George Schreiber, 1935

This makes him sound portentous. In his own personality, he wasn't, not in the least. He was cheerful, unaffected and amiable to everyone, and extremely witty. He was the best company of all the great physicists. In his serious moments, and there were many as the political scene darkened, he did speak from a depth of moral experience. He was as certain of his moral insight as of his physical insight. He wanted to do his best for his fellow humans, but he was the least sentimental of men. He recognized no collective loyalties except to the human race. He had renounced his German nationality at the age of sixteen, one of the most astonishing – and revealing – acts that any boy has ever done. But he wasn't really a boy – he was full of animal spirits and vigour, but his nature was formed at a very early age.

The laboratory at Zurich's Technische
Hochschule where Einstein performed many of
his earliest experiments

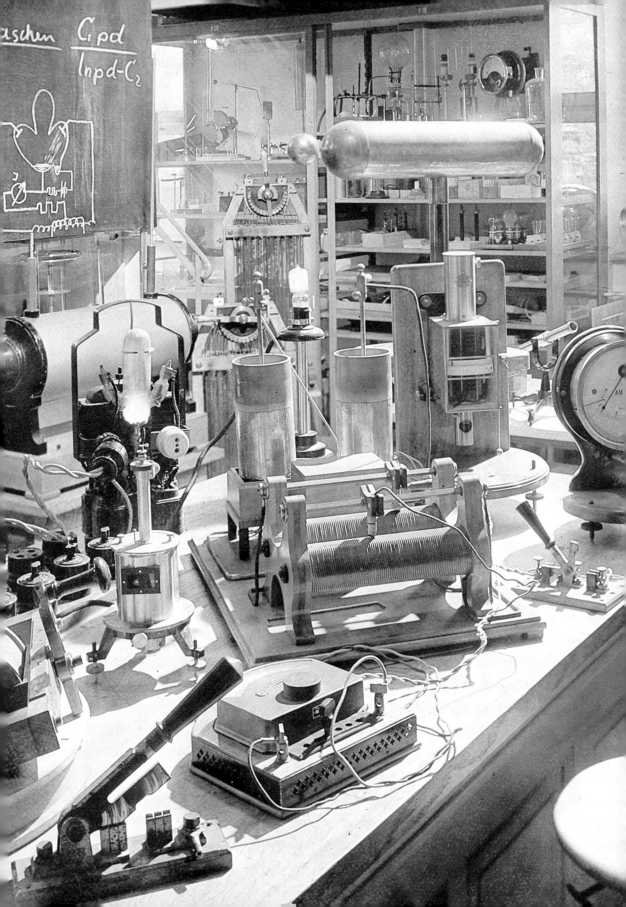

He had no use for the minute differences which divide men from one another. It is true that, though he didn't believe in Judaism any more than he believed in any other religion, he preserved a special feeling for his own Jewish people. Conversely, while he was given all honours in Germany and the conditions for his major achievement, he does seem to have had a special negative feeling for Germans. In later life he did not admit to having made a real German friend – outside German Jews. That was odd, in one so benevolent and so removed from ordinary human rancour. But, though he was as much above pettiness of spirit as anyone, he was human after all.

Einstein was not deeply interested in the details of particle physics. Max Planck had shown in 1900 that light is emitted in distinct 'packets' or quanta of energy (a concept essential for the later theory of modern physics, though undervalued by some historians of science), and Einstein's 1905 paper on the photo-electric effect added the significant point that light remains in these packets as it travels. But after that he went off, single-minded, in his own cosmic thoughts. No one has ever been able to think more obsessively, and for longer, on a single issue. It was a supreme gift for his kind of abstract creation – perhaps for any other creation – and one he shared, to the same degree, with his greatest predecessor, Newton.

Of course, he read what was being discovered about the structure of the atom. He said later, in his benign manner, that he had been impressed by the beauty of Rutherford's experiments, done with the simplest of means,

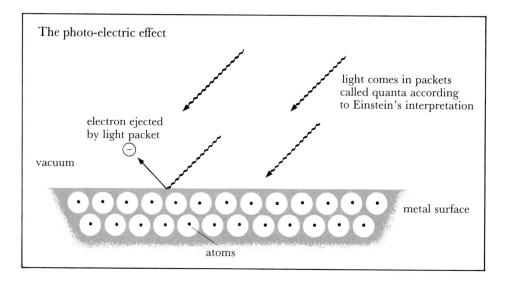

The photo-electric effect

light comes in packets called quanta according to Einstein's interpretation

electron ejected by light packet

vacuum

metal surface

atoms

Einstein in conversation with Dr Ludendorf, brother of
the famous general. Both were directors of the Potsdam
Astrophysical Laboratory

and going straight for physical reality. Einstein wished, so he said, that he
had been able to write something about Rutherford in his own work, but
there hadn't been any adequate connection.

That may not have been more than a handsome gesture to another
great figure. Rutherford tried to reciprocate, announcing in a speech that
the General Theory of Relativity, irrespective of whether it was valid, was
a magnificent work of art.

The qualification in that tribute has an eloquence of its own.

Rutherford knew perfectly well that the General Theory was valid, but
he didn't believe that it added much to his own idea of physics. The two

men never became close. They made speeches together when in 1933 Rutherford was leading a campaign to find aid for Jewish scientific refugees. But Rutherford didn't make an attempt to attract Einstein to Cambridge. It wasn't necessary: Einstein, as everyone knew, was receiving offers from all over America, Britain, Europe, and in his casual good-natured manner was tending to accept them all.

The trouble between the two was caused, at least in part, by the disparity in the treatment of the great experimentalists as contrasted with that of the great theoreticians.

In terms of popular esteem, experimentalists felt, and still feel, as Rutherford did with his usual horse-power, that they got an unfair deal. The names of theoreticians survived in intellectual currency: the names of experimentalists didn't. Einstein provided the most vivid illustration.

Before he was forty, with the General Theory still waiting for a conclusive experimental test, Einstein was the most famous scientist in the world – perhaps more famous than any scientist would be again. Whereas Rutherford had nothing but celebrity amongst scientists themselves. He might have taken the first great steps in elucidating the structure of the atom, but he wasn't a national figure, not celebrated as a film star in the way that Einstein was. Experimentalists did all the ground work, and without the results of experiments there wouldn't be any theory. Yet no experimentalist had ever caught the popular imagination. Inventors had, occasionally, witness Edison and Marconi, but never scientists doing experiments to discover the fundamentals of the universe.

It seemed mysterious. It was as though popular opinion had somehow realized that science, the whole great enterprise, was a collective activity in which individual personalities, and individual achievements, didn't much matter. If one practitioner didn't make a discovery this year, someone else would come along and make it next year. And that was true at the height of scientific creativity. If Rutherford hadn't proved the existence of the atom's nucleus in 1911, no one doubts that someone would have performed the same experiments within a decade, probably less than that.

A great scientist adds his own brick to the cumulative edifice. There are few human beings who have the capacity to be great scientists. It was once estimated that only one person in a million could do first-class original work, and that was drawing the line far below the Rutherfords. Nevertheless, if one scientist doesn't add his appropriate brick, another will.

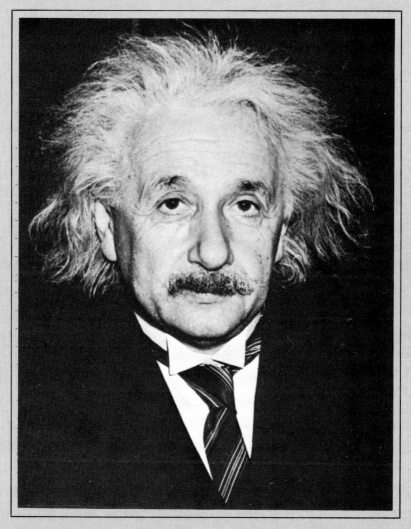

Einstein in his later years, 'a benign deity who had a
considerable resemblance to a handsome and inspired golliwog'

H. J. G. Moseley, one of the rising stars of English science, was killed at
Gallipoli, aged twenty-seven. He had had time to leave an indelible mark
on the text books: if he had lived, he would have been one of the very great.
And yet, though he would have done splendid things, those things in due
course were inexorably done by others, and the sand smoothed down over
Moseley's absence as though he had never been.

Much of those sobering thoughts applies to theoreticians also – but not
quite so bleakly. First of all, great theoreticians are even rarer animals
than great experimentalists. That kind of conceptual skill is one of the
most uncommon of all human gifts. Perhaps one in a hundred million is
born with the potential to be something like Clerk Maxwell, and even that
guess may be over-optimistic. As a consequence, their creations are not
quite so quickly replaceable. The most incisive tribute to Einstein was
made by Dirac, who doesn't inflate his words. Dirac said first that if
Einstein hadn't published the Special Theory of Relativity in 1905, someone else would have done it within an extremely short time, five years or
less. Several people, we now know, were already very near, Lorentz,
Minkowski, Poincaré: that is exactly like the standard position in experimental physics.

But, Dirac went on, the General Theory, which Einstein published in
1916, is an entirely different matter. Without it, it is likely that we should
still be waiting for the theory today. That is one of the most striking things
ever said of one great scientist by another.

There was no injustice in Einstein's transcending fame. Still it is
possible that the *mana* of his personality encouraged it. He was so unlike
the rest of human kind. Amusing, more than a bit of a deliberate clown;
unshakable, supremely confident both in scientific and moral judgements.
When he felt deeply, he was rather like an Old Testament prophet, or else
a benign deity being patient with human stupidity and worse – but also
like a benign deity who had considerable physical resemblance to a
handsome and inspired golliwog. No one who knew him expected to meet
anything like that again: and they were right.

Whether Rutherford felt anything like that about him, we don't know.
In spite of the aura around Einstein, his scientific thinking was as direct as
Rutherford's own. But it might not have reconciled Rutherford to
theoreticians in general, and to this one theoretician in particular, to be
told so.

4
The quiet Dane

Niels Bohr opening the Nordic summer university in 1951

There was, however, one theoretical physicist who became an intimate of Rutherford, and with whom there was mutual admiration and something like love, paternal on Rutherford's side, filial on the other. This was Niels Bohr. Towards the end of 1911, Bohr came diffidently into Rutherford's laboratory office in Manchester. They had met briefly before, but this was the first time Bohr had obtruded himself; obtrude perhaps isn't a good description of Bohr's behaviour – punctilious, excessively sensitive, eager to show his homage to a great man. Bohr was a Dane, then twenty-six years old, tall, with an enormous domed head, and much more muscular and athletic than his cautious manner suggested.

He was in trouble. He had been having a bad time in Cambridge, having spent months in the Cavendish trying to extract some interest from J. J. Thomson. Thomson had been bright and polite, as he usually was, had invited Bohr to dinner at Trinity, but had failed to show interest in his ideas. Bohr had brought his latest paper (actually a work of much originality), but in spite of many tactful hints Thomson hadn't shown any inclination to read it. It remained among the pile of manuscripts on Thomson's desk waiting for the attention which they never seemed to get. Bohr persisted, having a good deal of gentle Nordic stoicism, but after months he gave up. He left the old luminary and went to see if he could get some sympathy from the rising one. (Incidentally, Thomson had the unfortunate distinction of losing for the Cavendish both Rutherford and Bohr, founders of modern physics.)

Rutherford liked Bohr at sight. Patiently he listened. It says much for his judgement not only of scientific ability, but of men, that he formed a high opinion of Bohr on the spot, and one that never wavered.

Rutherford listened. The explication took a long time and Rutherford was by temperament not at all a patient man. But he stuck it out, and that is another tribute to his judgement – and perhaps to his kindness, for he saw that the young man was unhappy.

Niels Bohr, the diffident genius who founded modern
theoretical physics

THE ALUMINIUM ATOM

before Thomson
(solid billiard ball)

Rutherford 1911

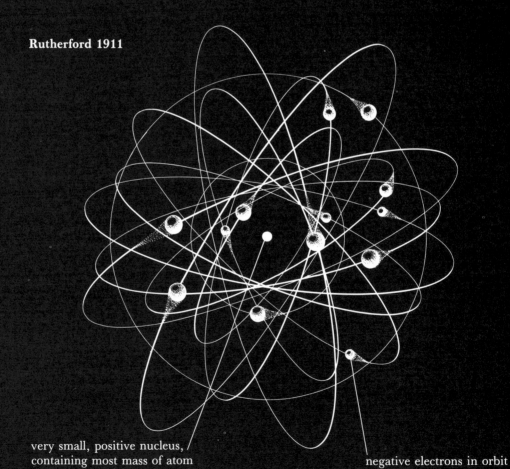

very small, positive nucleus,
containing most mass of atom

negative electrons in orbit

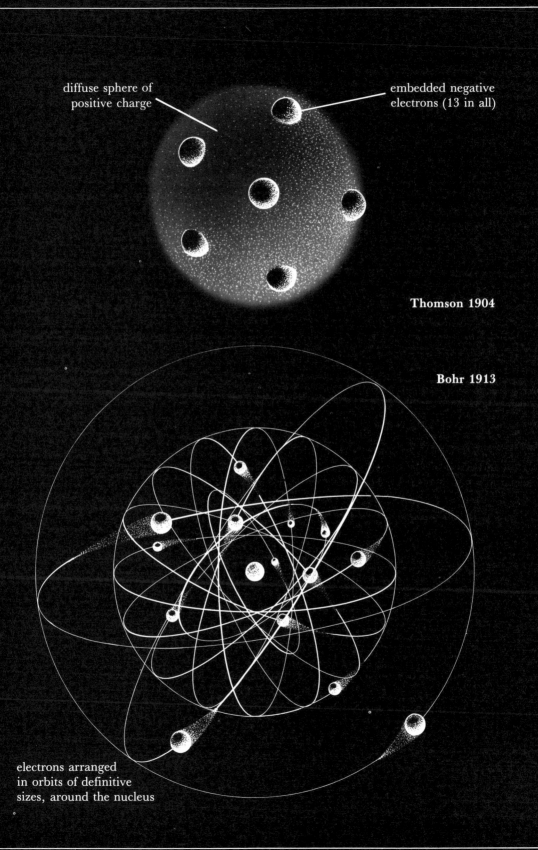

diffuse sphere of
positive charge

embedded negative
electrons (13 in all)

Thomson 1904

Bohr 1913

electrons arranged
in orbits of definitive
sizes, around the nucleus

In retrospect it is a nice scene. One has to remember Rutherford was loud-voiced and explosive and liked his own way in a conversation. With Bohr, even the young Bohr, he was unlikely to get it. For Bohr, though one of the deepest minds of his century, and the incarnation of altruism, was a talker as hard to get to the point as Henry James in his later years. One qualification sprang out of another. He had to dig down for the final, the perfect word, and, on not finding it, had pauses, minutes long, in which he reiterated a word which was clinging to his mind.

It didn't help that he spoke with a soft voice, not much above a whisper. Further, he was speaking to Rutherford in a language not his own. None of that deterred him. He was the most enthusiastic of talkers, whispering away, as he was to do for the next fifty years. He very much preferred talking to writing. On paper he was equally labyrinthine, and that took even more time as he, in search of the perfect expression, made draft after draft.

Not many acts of kindness and good judgement have had more creative results than that of Rutherford. Einstein wouldn't have needed encouragement: the young Bohr did. He stayed in Manchester, buoyed up by Rutherford's zest and his gift for communicating that he was usually right. Within two years Bohr, with his characteristic mixture of cautiousness and daring, produced a theoretical equivalent of Rutherford's nuclear atom, a theory as daring as it was original.

In Rutherford's model of the atom, electrons orbited the central nucleus, held in by its electrical attraction, in much the same way as the planets are held in orbit about the sun by its gravitational pull. It explained his experiments neatly. Unfortunately, the laws of classical physics did not allow Rutherford's atom to exist. According to the electromagnetic theory which Maxwell had built on the foundations laid by Faraday, an electrically charged particle produces radiation if it is diverted from a straight path. The electrons in Rutherford's atom were in circular orbits, so they should have been radiating all the time. If they did so, they would be losing energy, and would have spiralled down into the nucleus in a fraction of a second. The atom would have collapsed on itself.

Rutherford was not perturbed: he was not a theoretician. It was Bohr who provided the theoretical backbone. Without contradicting Maxwell in the general run of physics, he simply asserted that when an electron is orbiting a nucleus it does not radiate. This made no sense in classical physics. But it worked. For Bohr was bold enough to include a second assumption which meant his new theory could explain the long-standing puzzle of the pattern of wavelengths – spectral lines – from hydrogen.

Planck and Einstein had shown, years before, that light travels with certain energies, in packets called 'quanta'. The energy of a quantum is related to the wavelength of the light in question. Nineteenth-century physicists had found that each element produces a characteristic spectrum of light: it emits light of only particular wavelengths. In the twentieth-century view, this meant that each type of atom produces only light quanta of particular energy – but until Bohr's theory of the atom, no one had any idea why.

Bohr's second assumption was that electrons cannot orbit the nucleus in just any old orbit. The radius – and so the energy – of the permissible orbits was determined by a number that came out of Planck's earlier work, a number known to physicists as Planck's Constant. When an electron was in a permissible orbit, it circled around the nucleus without emitting light (or any other radiation). But an electron could spontaneously jump from one permissible orbit to another. As it did so, it either absorbed light (going 'uphill'), or emitted light (coming 'downhill'). Bohr calculated the permissible orbits for the simplest element, hydrogen, which has only one

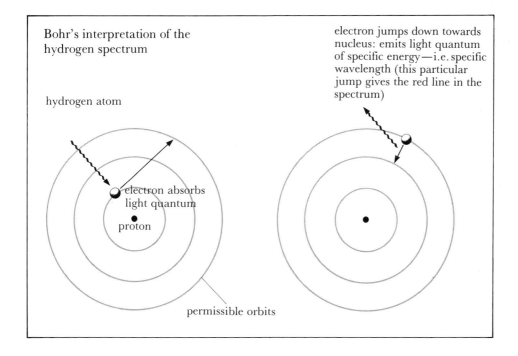

Bohr's interpretation of the hydrogen spectrum

hydrogen atom

electron jumps down towards nucleus: emits light quantum of specific energy—i.e. specific wavelength (this particular jump gives the red line in the spectrum)

electron absorbs light quantum

proton

permissible orbits

electron. He then worked out what energies were involved in an electron jumping from one permissible orbit to another. Assuming that this energy was converted into light, he calculated the corresponding wavelengths. He compared these to the known, and long puzzling, spectrum of hydrogen. The match was exact.

This was the first success of quantum theory in the field that classical physics had always regarded as its own: the physics of matter. From 1913 on, theoreticians knew the limits of classical physics on the very small scale. Bohr's quantum description of the hydrogen atom explained in brilliant and precise detail the spectrum lines of hydrogen, previously a blinding mystery. The nineteenth century had accumulated beautifully observed spectra of many elements, all of which had been as incomprehensible as Etruscan. When Einstein heard of how the theory matched so strongly with the data of the spectrum lines, he said, with delight and wonder: 'Then this is one of the greatest discoveries.'

Very soon Bohr, still a youngish man, became the father of atomic theory. He became director of the Institute for Theoretical Physics,

Bohr in the laboratory of his new Institute

Opposite: Front page of the Copenhagen daily *Politiken* when Bohr received the Nobel prize for physics in 1922

designed for him and by him, in Copenhagen, a centre unlike any other in the history of physics. For theoreticians it was both duty and pleasure to attend there, just to hear Bohr talk – talk at considerable length, but also with questions tentative and probing, not sharp or witty, but moving circuitously and patiently towards a new truth. Tough-minded scientists, not over given to respect, used to come back from Copenhagen and report – in that idyllic age of physics – that Bohr was doing it all.

They liked to call his method Socratic, but they didn't know those ancient dialogues very well. It was really different in kind, the chief resemblance being that Socrates wrote nothing and Bohr surprisingly little. Historians of science are going to find a puzzle in identifying exactly what he did. There is one good biography, but nothing like the mass of literature written around Einstein, alive or dead.

Bohr's personality hadn't the effortless power of Einstein's and he hadn't the devil-may-care attitude and the emphatic tongue. He didn't convey, as Einstein did, the immediate presence of moral experience. But he did suggest brooding wisdom and, above all, selfless concern. More than almost any creative man of the highest calibre, he didn't have a hard ego off which others bounced as from a billiard ball. He was not, as Einstein was, impersonally kind to the human race; he was simply and genuinely kind. It sounds insipid, but in addition to wisdom he had much sweetness. He was a loving and beloved husband and father.

The 'Copenhagen school' was a creation of his personality as well as his intellect. He had certain extra advantages. It was a help that he came from a small neutral country, had no national prejudices and evoked none. An American or Russian Bohr, or even an English or French one, would have caused more superficial impediments. Also he had a peculiarly propitious family background. His father had been a professor of physiology at Copenhagen, his grandfather an academic also; and one of his sons now occupies Niels's old position. They were a high-minded academic family, in some ways similar to those the English have been used to – but appreciably more liberal, more conscious of a sense of moral duty, and very much more cultivated. The Bohrs had all read widely in at least four languages, applied themselves to philosophy as well as to literature, become lovers of music and the visual arts. They were as educated as it is possible to become in this century of ours. Without any of them realizing it, some of this civilization spun off. A good many young men couldn't help the vestigial thought that this was what the intellectual life ought to be; just as those did, though there were far fewer, who came close to Einstein, himself cultivated in a good Central European fashion, with strong creative feelings about books and music, feelings more positive than Bohr's. In the clash which was to come a few years later in the late 1920s, right at the climactic point of modern physics, it wasn't Einstein's classical clarity which prevailed, but Bohr's delicate nosing his way among the contradictions of the natural world. Clash is too bleak a word for a debate, as profound as any in intellectual history, between two such deep-minded men. The disagreement was about ultimate things, and expressed the mysteries, as well as the triumphs, of the scientific world picture.

5
The golden age

One of Rutherford's experiments in 1923. An alpha
particle strikes a helium nucleus and they part at right angles

For a period of ten years – which included the First World War – there was something like a muddle, as scientists argued about the Rutherford-Bohr atom. Not on the side of experimentalists. Rutherford went indomitably ahead, come war, come theorists (Bohr excepted, to whom he confided any startling result), come philosophers (dismissed under the general Rutherfordian heading of 'those fellows'). Rutherford's experiments, still masterly in their simplicity (brutally simple, the over-sophisticated felt), were having an earthquake-like success. In 1919, he started firing alpha particles at nitrogen atoms. Nothing much should have happened. A great deal did.

As in his earlier experiments, the alpha particles came from radium. This time he was directing them down a tube filled with nitrogen gas. At the far end, he found he was detecting not just alpha particles, but also particles with all the properties of hydrogen nuclei. There was, however, no hydrogen in the tube. With his high-speed alpha-particle projectiles, Rutherford had actually broken them off the nuclei of the nitrogen atoms.

The discovery of radioactivity had earlier shown that certain, rare types of atom could spontaneously disintegrate. Now Rutherford had shown that ordinary atoms were not indestructible. By knocking out a hydrogen nucleus (later called a proton) from the nucleus of nitrogen he had converted it into another element, oxygen. Rutherford had, to a limited extent, achieved the dream of the alchemists and changed one element to another.

With Chadwick, Rutherford spent the next five years breaking up the nuclei of another ten elements, using alpha-particle projectiles. These experiments didn't leave much room for argument. And as well as the philosophical implication of changing elements, the Rutherford-Chadwick experiments showed that the nuclei of atoms could be probed. They were not just positively charged, dense balls of matter: they must have some kind of internal structure.

That was an experimental conquest. Meanwhile, the understanding of the arrangement of electrons in the outer part of the atom hadn't made much progress. Einstein took a hand. He calculated just how bright the different spectral lines from Bohr's atom should be (producing a formula which later led to the development of the laser). He was also developing a new kind of statistics to deal with sub-atomic particles, following a proposal by the Indian physicist, Satyendra Bose. On the philosophical front, Einstein was gently insisting on the classical axiom – that if you knew everything about a present physical situation, you could predict everything about its future. At their first meeting, Bohr was already, though polite and deferential, in his brooding, inexplicit fashion feeling dubious. That interchange cast its shadow before it.

The fact was, there was no satisfactory theory of the atom. Bohr's model explained the simplest atom, hydrogen, brilliantly, but it totally failed when confronted by the spectra of other elements. Clearly the situation was much more complicated when atoms had more than one electron. And even in the case of hydrogen, Bohr had simply made two assumptions without any theoretical backing. There was no kind of logical rigour. There was, however, plenty of opportunity for experiment, enough to keep 'particle physics' – as the science of probing the ever-smaller was becoming known – bounding along. Rutherford moved from Manchester to succeed Thomson in the Cavendish Chair at Cambridge in 1919, and immediately collected many of the future galaxy. That was when Kapitsa began studying the professor's temperament and when Chadwick clinched Rutherford's experiments on the first human-directed nuclear disintegration. In Copenhagen Bohr was, with his customary thoroughness, supervising all details of his new institute. He didn't leave architecture, any more than his verbal statements, to chance.

Cambridge and Copenhagen were set to lead the new atomic physics, bound by the personal ties of Rutherford and Bohr, and by the functional ties of Copenhagen theory and Cambridge experiment. But there still wasn't a fundamental solution to the problem of the atom's structure, certainly not one which would satisfy any kind of mathematical inspection. A third plinth was needed. It came in what still seems a fantastically short time. It came from Germany.

At this time, physicists wanted to know how the electrons in an atom were arranged, what governed their energies and motions. Although Rutherford and Chadwick had begun to probe the central nucleus, most

Bohr's Institute for Theoretical Physics in Copenhagen

scientists were content to let its problems rest until the structure of the orbiting electrons was worked out. It needed someone to look at the observable facts with a fresh eye.

There was no way of directly 'seeing' an atom. But as Bohr had pointed out, the spectrum of light from an element was speaking of energy changes within the atom as electrons moved from one permissible state (orbits in Bohr's model) to another. Every element produces its own characteristic set of distinct wavelengths of light, forming 'lines' in the spectrum. And most are far more complex than the spectrum of hydrogen.

Experimentalists could probe atomic structure further, by perturbing the electrons with magnetic fields and electric fields. When atoms of an element were put between the poles of a powerful magnet, or between electrically charged plates, the spectrum altered slightly. Each spectral line split up into a number of closely spaced lines, each of slightly different wavelength.

As if all this wealth of unexplained detail from spectra wasn't enough, the energy needed to knock electrons out of atoms could be measured by

Theory of structure of atom

Suppose atom consists of + charge ne at centre + − charge as electrons distributed throughout sphere of radius b.

Force at p on electron $= Ne^2 \left\{ \dfrac{1}{r^2} - \dfrac{r^3}{b^3} \cdot \dfrac{1}{r^2} \right\}$

$$= Ne^2 \left\{ \dfrac{1}{r^2} - \dfrac{r}{b^3} \right\} \quad = \quad \not A \; \not\ast$$

Suppose charged particle e mass m moves through atom so that deflection is small. Let $\perp^r$ distance from centre $= a$

Deflecting force $\perp^r$ direction function at p
$$= Ne^2 \left\{ \dfrac{1}{r^2} - \dfrac{r}{b^3} \right\} \cos\theta$$

∴ accel $\perp^r$ direction function $= d\alpha = \dfrac{Ne^2}{m} \left\{ \dfrac{1}{r^2} - \dfrac{r}{b^3} \right\} \dfrac{a}{r}$

∴ Velocity u acquired in passing through atom $\perp^r$ direction

$$u = \int d\alpha \cdot dt = Ne \int d\alpha \cdot \dfrac{ds}{V}$$

$$= \dfrac{Ne^2}{mV} \int_b \left(\dfrac{1}{r^2} - \dfrac{r}{b^3} \right) \dfrac{a}{r} \cdot \dfrac{r\,dr}{\sqrt{r^2 - a^2}}$$

$$= 2 \dfrac{Ne^2}{mV} \int_0 \dfrac{a(b^3 - r^3)}{r^2 b^3} \dfrac{dr}{\sqrt{r^2 - a^2}} \quad \left\{ \dfrac{1}{r^2} - \dfrac{r}{b^3} \right\} \cdot \dfrac{dr}{\sqrt{r^2 - a^2}}$$

$$= \dfrac{2 Ne^2}{mV} \int \dfrac{\cos^2\theta \cos^2\theta}{a} - \dfrac{a^2}{b^3 \cos\theta} \dfrac{\sin\theta}{a \sin\theta \cos\theta} \cos\theta \quad r = \dfrac{a}{\cos\theta}$$

Paul Dirac and Werner Heisenberg in 1933

shooting at them with fast electrons in a nearly evacuated tube. It was a sophisticated version of the old cathode ray experiments. Except that now the experimenters were not interested in the cathode rays themselves: these electrons were just bullets to attack the atoms of gas left in the tube.

The experiments had gathered a tremendous harvest of observable facts – too tremendous for comfort. Bohr's simple intuitive model for hydrogen just could not cope; all rough and ready constructions had to be swept away before a complete theory of the atom could emerge. Was a physical picture of the atom even necessary? Perhaps one could write down a purely mathematical representation of the atom, without thinking of individual electrons moving in orbits at all.

On this view, each type of atom would have a particular set of numbers associated with it. Then there would be rules to calculate its observable properties. For example, you want to know the wavelengths of sodium's spectral lines? Apply the 'spectral lines' rule to a set of numbers corresponding to sodium, and the wavelengths will drop out. You can apply this same rule to the mathematical representation of sulphur, and out will come its spectral line wavelengths. To work out how sodium's spectral lines are split up by a magnetic field, apply another rule – the 'Zeeman effect' rule – to the set of numbers describing sodium. And so on.

There's no point in talking about things you can't measure directly – like electron orbits. Write down mathematical formulations that relate directly to the observable facts. That was the thought of a very young man of genius, Werner Heisenberg, who had both physical and mathematical insight ready to burst out to the highest degree. The trouble was, he didn't know enough of the curiosities of nineteenth-century mathematics, when all kinds of mathematical arts had been developed. Not for use, but for the sheer beauty of the game.

Fortunately there was a slightly older theoretician at Göttingen who was not only gifted but had had the most thorough of German mathematical educations. This was Max Born. He told Heisenberg, like someone pointing to a paragraph in a newspaper, that there was no problem. The old subject of matrix algebra, half forgotten but completely available, would give them precisely what they needed. A 'matrix' is a two-dimensional table of numbers, and in 1859 the English mathematician Arthur Cayley had devised rules by which two matrices can be 'multiplied' together to give another matrix. In Heisenberg's scheme, each atom would be represented by a matrix; each 'rule' by another matrix. If one multiplied the 'sodium' matrix by the 'spectral lines' matrix this should give the matrix of wavelengths of sodium's spectral lines. And it did. Heisenberg was a natural mathematician, and it took him only a few days to assimilate matrix algebra. Born knew as much mathematics as any physicist alive. They co-opted another clever young man, Pascual Jordan, and completed a paper on matrix mechanics, the foundation of the new atomic theory, in less than a month.

Thus Göttingen took the lead in the new theory. It became known as quantum mechanics. For the first time, atomic structure had a genuine, though very surprising, mathematical base. The climate of Göttingen was in the highest tradition of German scientific thinking. This was then familiar to the whole of academic Europe. Only ten years or so earlier, that is before the 1914–18 war, Englishmen regularly went to Germany for their graduate work. Germany had been, in many fields including mathematics, the centre of the academic world. The English had been amateurs, sometimes gifted amateurs, playing with professionals. Born and Heisenberg came straight from the élite of German academic life. Remarkably like Bohr in Denmark, both came from talented families. Their fathers had occupied distinguished Professorial Chairs before them. They were steeped in the culture, wide and deep, which had somehow escaped their English counterparts. Literature and music were part of the air they had always breathed. Born was Jewish on both sides; he was also a splendid example of German liberal civilization at its most refined.

There was one singularity. The general atmosphere of the three plinths of atomic physics in 1925 was vaguely liberal, strongly international, pacific, often apolitical. That last was specially true of the Cavendish. The young Heisenberg, though he didn't obtrude his opinions, was an odd man out. He was an active man, a good games player, fond of the physical life; not a bit like the stereotype of an asthenic conceptual thinker. He was pure German, not Jewish. He was, quietly, a German nationalist. As a student, he had belonged to one of the nationalist organizations – not the Nazis, who would have been too crude at that period for a young man of his calibre. All this had consequences twenty years later. The level of intellectual excitement in 1925, however, was so high that interest in others' opinions outside science was correspondingly low. And anyway, that kind of personal perception wasn't a necessary quality among high-class scientists.

Max Born (seated) and his colleagues at Göttingen's *Bohr Festspiele* in June 1922. Behind him, left to right, are William Osler, Niels Bohr, James Franck and Oscar Klein

The level of intellectual excitement ran even higher, when another theory arrived out of the blue. On the face of it, this theory appeared to have nothing in common with quantum mechanics. The maddening thing was, it also worked. It also happened in 1925, the cardinal year of atomic physics. In Paris, Louis de Broglie (who was a member of a suitably Proustian ducal family), working entirely on his own account, proposed that if atomic particles were regarded simultaneously as waves, some pleasant simplification and explanation would follow.

The idea was completely novel. Like nearly all the best ideas, it wasn't elaborate. It simply hadn't occurred to others. Planck and Einstein had shown that light – always regarded as a kind of wave – could sometimes act as if it was a 'solid' particle carrying a certain amount of energy (a quantum). Now de Broglie was saying that particles – like electrons, or even whole atoms – could sometimes behave like waves. Experiments quickly proved he was right. The wave-particle duality of matter is not easy to grasp intuitively, though. Exact interpretations varied from scientist to scientist, but it's easiest to think of an electron (for example) being a particle with a 'guiding wave'. Classical wave phenomena happen to these guiding waves, like interference where the troughs and crests of two waves can cancel out. The intensity of the wave at any point indicates how likely you are to find the electron there.

Despite its apparent oddness, the idea of de Broglie waves immediately caught on. Erwin Schrödinger, an Austrian of much intellectual power, set to work to give meaning, and mathematical articulation, to the de Broglie waves. He applied them to the electrons in atoms, and found that they explained as much as the quantum mechanical descriptions. The mathematics was more commonplace, and easier to handle.

Take the hydrogen atom for example. Schrödinger thought of the electron in its orbit not as a miniature planet, but as a wave – like the wiggles in a rope when you jerk the end up and down. But the electron rope is tied right round the nucleus. It has no end. To think of it another way, the two ends are tied together, so as it vibrates the two 'ends' must move with one another. This means there must be a whole number of 'wiggles' (electron wavelengths) in the rope. There could be one, two, ten – but not $2\frac{1}{2}$, $3\frac{2}{3}$ – because then one 'end' would not be moving with the other. So the Schrödinger atom has electrons only at certain distances from the nucleus, where the circumference of their path is a whole number of electron wavelengths. And using de Broglie's formula for the

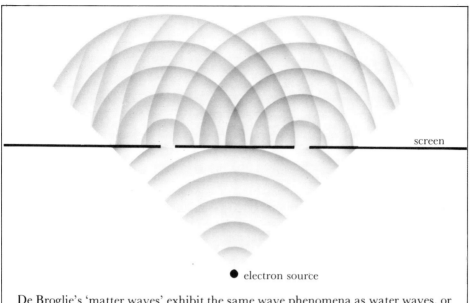

screen

● electron source

De Broglie's 'matter waves' exhibit the same wave phenomena as water waves, or light – for example, interference. When light passes through a double slit, the two new expanding wavefronts 'interfere' to produce regions of intense disturbance (bright) and relative calm (darkness). Matter behaves similarly, but on a much smaller scale: disturbed – high energy – regions of 'matter waves' show where the matter particle is most likely to be

wavelength, Schrödinger found his permissible electron paths were exactly those that Bohr had found from his assumptions. The reason for Bohr's permissible orbits turned out to lie in the wave-nature of matter. But the Schrödinger theory not only explained Bohr's hydrogen atom; it successfully predicted the properties of other atoms.

The Schrödinger-de Broglie method was utterly different both in spirit and form from quantum mechanics. Yet both arrived at the same result; both could explain the observed facts equally well. Impasse. Confusion. The best conceptual minds in physics argued away: which was right? Then, to the general relief, there was anticlimax. Schrödinger demonstrated that the two formulations were equivalent. Although matter waves and matrices seem so different, they were only different mathematical ways of saying the same thing. You could use whichever you wanted, and change from one to the other. The physicists were happy that they had the explanation, at last a mathematically sound atomic theory, in their hands.

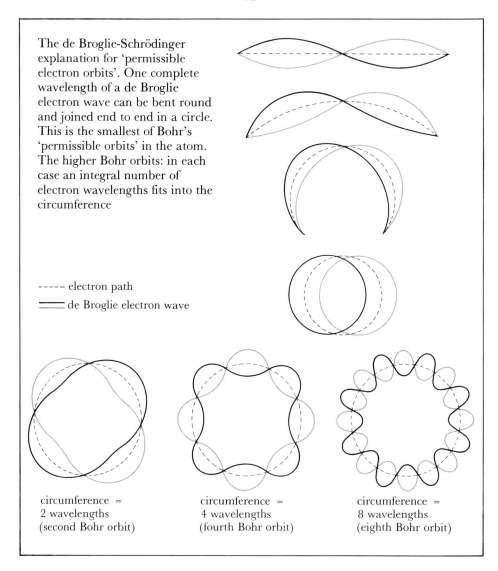

The de Broglie-Schrödinger explanation for 'permissible electron orbits'. One complete wavelength of a de Broglie electron wave can be bent round and joined end to end in a circle. This is the smallest of Bohr's 'permissible orbits' in the atom. The higher Bohr orbits: in each case an integral number of electron wavelengths fits into the circumference

----- electron path

===== de Broglie electron wave

circumference = 2 wavelengths (second Bohr orbit)

circumference = 4 wavelengths (fourth Bohr orbit)

circumference = 8 wavelengths (eighth Bohr orbit)

Heisenberg then produced one of the most dramatic of all physical concepts. It became known as the Uncertainty Principle – meaning that the exact position and precise velocity of an electron could not be determined at the same time. Which meant something more disturbing – that, in the sub-atomic world, causality broke down. It would never (literally never) be possible to predict exactly where an individual electron would be. The only statements that could be made, and this was as far as human

Schrödinger's interpretation of the atom, 1925. The intensity of shading shows the *probability* of finding an electron at any point in the atom

Energy level diagram showing how the 13 electrons of an aluminium atom are distributed between the allowed 'shells' (or 'orbitals')

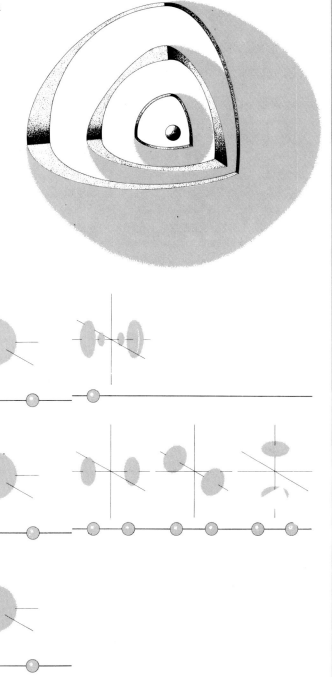

energy of electron

3rd shell

2nd shell

1st shell
(innermost)

electrons in spherical shells   electrons in 'double-lobe' shells

minds could reach, were statistical. For an individual electron, one could only say where it was *likely* to be. Detailed predictions were valid for assemblies of large numbers of particles, not for one. This became the final ground of the Einstein-Bohr debate a few years later, a debate which continued until the end of Einstein's life.

In the late 1920s, the masters of theoretical physics had reached a peak of achievement and confidence (Einstein dissenting). It was possible to say – it was said by some with the most critical minds – that the fundamental laws of physics and chemistry were now laid down for ever. That wasn't a boast. Though there have been qualifications since, those laws are now part of the scientific edifice – the most successful of the collective works of the human intellect.

It is true some of the laws when first enunciated appeared bizarre. But wise men said that, within a generation, those laws would become familiar, part of the common scientific language, as taken for granted as those of Maxwell or Newton. That has been demonstrated, now that time has passed. Any competent student today accepts the Uncertainty Principle as a matter of course; and knows about the most beautiful creation of that extraordinary epoch in scientific history. Here I refer to the culmination of wave mechanics, quantum mechanics and atomic structure, in the work of Dirac.

Dirac crowned the achievement of that marvellous decade by combining all the ideas of de Broglie, Schrödinger, Heisenberg and Born with the relativity theory of Einstein. Physicists had been totally preoccupied with sorting out atomic structure. Though they knew that relativity had to be included somehow, it wasn't obvious how. Dirac pulled all the strings together in 1928, and showed that incorporating relativity removed the last of the atom's puzzles. It explained quite naturally the rather odd fact that individual electrons spin around on their own axes, like miniature tops, as they orbit within the atom.

In the judgement of the most accomplished pure mathematicians, Dirac, of all the theoretical physicists, was the one who had, in mathematics itself, the greatest elegance and power. He also had intense physical insight, but that pure mathematicians were not concerned with. He ought to have been a real mathematician, they said, rather as English soldiers regretted that Joan of Arc had the bad luck not to be one of them.

Dirac was English by birth, the only representative of his nationality to play a major part in this explosion of theoretical physics. As a matter of biographical history, his father was a Swiss, who had migrated to England and become a language teacher at a Bristol grammar school. Paul Dirac was brought up bilingually in French and English: with the curious consequence that he turned out abnormally taciturn in both languages. When he did express himself, however, it was with the absolute precision that distinguished all his thinking.

Symbols were Dirac's natural medium, and from a very early age – before he was three, which is about par for future mathematicians of the highest conceptual gifts – he was playing with mathematical ideas, such as the singular properties of infinite numbers. By what seems to have been sheer chance, he took his first degree in engineering. This didn't frustrate him unduly, since like Einstein in the Swiss patent office he showed a clear-eyed practical streak. But his ultimate gift was too remarkable to escape notice, quiet as he was. So he was duly propelled to Cambridge, and in his early twenties was publishing work which had clarity, originality and certitude. At that time there was only one Chair at Cambridge tenable by a mathematical physicist, and possible candidates were saying, without rancour, since genius of this order would have made rancour ridiculous, 'Oh well, there is no chance for us now.'

It was an illusion, commonly held, that all the greatest theoretical physicists were supreme mathematicians. That wasn't so. Physical insight was the necessary gift. Of course, they had no trouble with mathematical concepts. Dirac could have been any sort of mathematician, by the highest standards. Heisenberg had great natural ability, Bohr profound mathematical scholarship. But Einstein, who had been bored with mathematics as a student, had to pick up the techniques as he went along. Bohr hadn't anything like the mathematical facility of dozens of talented but lesser men – that may have been one reason why he chose his Socratic or conversational methods; and it may have inhibited him from producing the final formulation of the ideas of which, in the opinion of all round him, he was the originator.

Justice is hard to reach in any estimate of a collective enterprise. As well as the great names, there were many other men of talent milling round in those dazzling days of modern physics. It was a bit like the Elizabethan-Jacobean theatre. Then, anyone who could write at all could add something. The climate was right, the language was right, the conditions were all in favour. The major genius of Shakespeare, and perhaps the genius of another – Christopher Marlowe – would have triumphed in any period.

Others were lucky just to be borne along on the collective wave. That was so among the theoreticians of Göttingen and Copenhagen. One or two were slightly unlucky to be overshadowed by the Heisenbergs and Diracs.

An interesting character was Wolfgang Pauli, often invoked because of the edge of his critical intelligence. He was responsible for creative work of decisive significance. It is likely that in other times he would have stood out as a dominating figure. His major contribution was the Exclusion Principle, which explained why the electrons in an atom don't all drop down to the orbit (or energy level) closest to the nucleus: once an electron is in an orbit, it excludes any other from occupying the same orbit. As it is Pauli stands out in scientific legend, respected for the Exclusion Principle, but remembered for his viperish tongue. In the midst of so much gentleness and human acceptance, he was capable of savage sarcasm, very funny to those not on the receiving end. In literary terms, the Pauli comments were vastly preferable to the amiable strains of scientists' facetiousness.

That scientific explosion was a time of triumph and hope. Though there were shadows just apparent in the world outside, the international scene between 1925 and 1929 to most people still seemed sunny enough. Nearly all the scientists, if they thought of such things at all, looked forward to a peaceful future. They tended to expect other human beings to be as free from class and racial tensions as they were themselves. If the work was going well, it was good to be alive.

There was one oddity which didn't attract much attention at the time. If it had come to mind, it would have been dismissed as trivial. Theoretical physics, at this high point, was very much a Jewish science. Heisenberg wasn't Jewish, nor was Dirac or de Broglie. Almost all the other leading figures were. Bohr, the quintessence of Scandinavian virtue and the personification of Nordic manhood, had a Jewish mother. It would have seemed silly to wonder if this accidental fact about the physicists' origins was going to have its consequences.

6
The clouds gather

Students and Nazis burning books by foreign and Jewish authors in May 1933. The slogan on the truck reads 'German students march against the un-German intellect'

$-\frac{\hbar}{i}\frac{\partial}{\partial t} = \frac{p^2}{2m} - \frac{Ze^2}{r}$
$\alpha = \frac{\hbar^2}{ec}$
ϑ

The 1930s saw a convulsion in Europe which the scientists did not anticipate, and which then disrupted many of their lives. They were forced into the greatest emigration of intellectuals since the collapse of Byzantium, and one far more dramatic and influential than that. Einstein, himself homeless, had to help make provision for Jewish scientists now deprived. Rutherford gave a lead to the English scientific community. Bohr arranged for Copenhagen to be a staging post, though one too near to the Reich for any long-term safety. The Göttingen faculty was broken up. Born found himself in Edinburgh; others were scattered round American or British universities. Hungarians reaching the United States included a wildly clever trio, Wigner, Teller, Szilard, all three to have an extra significance in a few years' time. Hans Bethe arrived at Cornell. Men of high talent were grateful for comparatively humble posts.

Towards the end of the decade, just before the beginning of the war, a recent power in the scientific world, the Physics School in Rome, had to cross the Atlantic. Their leader, Enrico Fermi, was not himself Jewish, but had a Jewish wife. He had been recognized very young as one of the physicists of the century, and the only one who could work on equal terms with the greatest in both theory and experiment. There had been no one like that for generations. The great physicists of recent years had been either superb experimenters or gifted theoreticians: the two talents had not been combined in the same individual. If Fermi had been born thirty years earlier, it was possible to imagine him discovering Rutherford's nucleus, and then proceeding to Bohr's theory of the atom. If that sounds like hyperbole, anything said about Fermi is likely to sound hyperbolic. As a professional scientist, not as a cosmic thinker such as Einstein or Bohr, he was one of the very greatest.

The United States, because it was rich and because it was the most secure refuge (any Englishman had to advise German friends that these

Enrico Fermi, the Italian Nobel Laureate,
reached America in 1938

islands were uncomfortably near), received a high proportion of the Jewish scientists. It was the most significant influx of ability of which there is any record. America, of course, was already producing its native-born Nobel prize winners. The refugees made it, in a very short time, the world's dominant force in pure science. They also helped create what was soon called the Jewish explosion, a burst of creativity in all fields, not only science. There already existed native-born, or effectively native-born, American-Jewish physicists of world class, like the dazzling Rabi, who was to win the Nobel prize for his work on the magnetic properties of atoms. The refugees gave the explosion a new dynamic.

There were, needless to say, losses and tragedies in these transplant-ings. There must have been talent starved, most of which we shall never know. But physics, the physics of the 1920s, went on remarkably undis-turbed. Quantum mechanics as welded together by Dirac was now estab-lished as a final intellectual statement. As an aside, Einstein's argument with Bohr, whatever was happening to either of them, continued also undisturbed. At face value, quantum mechanics introduced uncertainty into the sub-atomic world: Heisenberg's Uncertainty Principle stated explicitly that it is impossible to measure precisely the position and velocity of an electron (or other particle) at the same moment. If so, it is then impossible to predict exactly where it will be at any time afterwards. In other words, a physicist could send off two electrons in the same direction, at the same speed – as precisely as he could – and they would not necessarily end up in the same place. In the language of classical physics, the same cause had produced different effects. The principle of causality was violated.

In the de Broglie-Schrödinger wave view of quantum mechanics, elec-trons are directed by a guiding wave. The intensity of the wave gives the probability of finding the electron. Even knowing the mathematical for-mulation of the wave precisely does not help the physicist predict an individual electron's position. A wave travelling through a narrow slit spreads out on the far side, like ocean waves entering a harbour. When electrons are shot through a slit, most will travel straight through. But the occasional incident electron, no different from any of the others, will be sent 'round the corner' by the guiding wave. Again, causality is violated. Although all the electrons entering the slit are identical, they end up going in different directions on the far side.

The Hungarian physicist Edward Teller found himself stranded
in the United States by events in Europe

Since the guiding wave pattern determines the probability of an electron going in a particular direction, the physicist can say where the bulk of the electrons will end up, and which regions behind the slit will be avoided. So he actually can make predictions when dealing with a large number of electrons. Precise causality has become a matter of statistics – just as a gambler can't predict he will throw a six when a die is rolled, but knows that if he rolls it often enough, a six will come up on one-sixth of the throws.

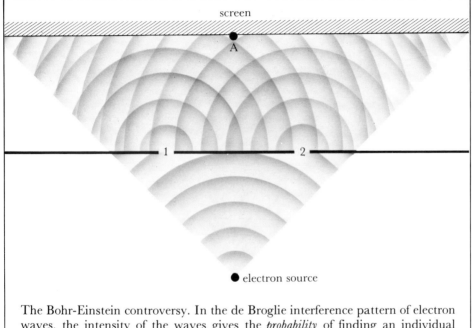

screen

A

1   2

● electron source

The Bohr-Einstein controversy. In the de Broglie interference pattern of electron waves, the intensity of the waves gives the *probability* of finding an individual electron. Bohr said the position of the electron only had meaning when it was detected – at A. It was impossible to know whether it came through slit 1 or 2 – indeed the question is meaningless. Einstein retorted that the electron must have followed a definite pattern, even if our present physics – limited by Heisenberg's Uncertainty Principle – can't tell us which slit it passed through

Some of the Manhattan project scientists at a reunion at the University of Chicago in 1946. Top row (left to right): N. Hilberry, Samuel Allison, Thomas Brill, Robert Nobles, Warren Nyer, Marvin Wilkening. Middle row: Harold Agnew, William Sturm, Harold Lichtenberger, Leona W. Marshall, Leo Szilard. Front row: Enrico Fermi, Walter Zinn, Albert Wattenberg, Herbert Anderson. With the influx of refugee scientists, the United States became the dominant force in physics

Was the sub-atomic world understandable only in terms of statistical chance? Bohr was certain of that ground. But perhaps quantum mechanics was just a temporary formulation, an approximation to deeper laws as yet undiscovered. These deeper laws could then be as strictly causal as those of the old classical physics. So argued Einstein. 'God doesn't play at dice,' he said with imperturbable conviction. Bohr, for once sharp-tongued, answered that he ought not to speak for what God (Bohr actually said Providence) could or could not do.

That was almost the only brusque exchange in the whole controversy. It was conducted with maximum generosity by both men. It was a model for any profound disagreement at the highest level. They respected and admired each other: each had no doubt that he was right. Incidentally, it was the deepest exploration of *how* we know things that has so far been conducted, and ought to be part of any course in academic philosophy. The whole weight of scientific opinion was beginning to come down in support of Bohr. It was only Einstein's transcendent authority that kept some of the argument open.

The passionate excitement in the physics of those years, however, took place elsewhere. There were a series of discoveries, all experimental, which were the most dramatic since Rutherford had proved, a dozen years before, that atomic nuclei could be disintegrated. To almost everyone these new discoveries seemed of absorbing scientific interest, giving the first dim insights into atomic nuclei; but the interest was the interest of pure science, nothing else but that.

The structure of the electrons in the outer part of the atom was now common knowledge amongst physicists. Whatever the philosophical status of quantum mechanics, it undoubtedly described how the electrons behaved. But little was known about the central nucleus. In the 1930s, physicists were to lay bare its mysteries with the same determination – and the same degree of success – as they had applied to the outer electrons in the previous two decades.

The year 1932 was one of scientific revelations. Rutherford had once predicted, with one of his direct intuitions backed by good firm reasoning, that a third sub-atomic particle must exist. The light-weight, negatively charged electrons were now old friends. The atomic nucleus must contain much heavier, positively charged particles. Physicists called them protons. According to Rutherford, there must exist another particle, as heavy as the proton, but having no electrical charge.

Such a neutral particle would possess great carrying power once it was on the move. With no electrical charge, its motion could not be altered by the electrical charge of an atomic nucleus. It could be stopped only by direct collision. There actually was some evidence from disintegration experiments that such particles existed: but it was necessary to know what one was looking for. In Paris, the great tradition of the Curies continued in the hands of their daughter Irène. She had married the Curies' assistant, Frédéric Joliot, and they combined their names, as they did their research. The Joliot-Curies had evidence for Rutherford's neutral particle in their own experiments, but they had mistakenly interpreted it as a kind of penetrating radiation.

But Chadwick knew what he was looking for. He calculated just what effects would distinguish a neutral particle from radiation. And then he set up experiments of classical beauty and simplicity to look for these effects. Like the Joliot-Curies, he shot alpha particles at a target of the light metal beryllium; and out came the mysterious 'radiation'. But Chadwick intercepted it with paraffin wax. The 'radiation' hit the nuclei of hydrogen atoms within the paraffin wax, and ejected *them* at high speed. Now the nucleus of hydrogen is none other than a single proton. By his measurements on the ejected protons, Chadwick proved that what was hitting them was not radiation: it was a neutral particle, almost identical in mass to the proton.

Chadwick, under a repressed façade, had the most acute of aesthetic senses and was an artist among the experimental physicists. He worked, night and day, for about three weeks. The dialogue passed into Cavendish tradition: 'Tired, Chadwick?' 'Not too tired to work.' And at the end, when he told his colleagues what he had done in one of the shortest accounts ever made about a major discovery: 'Now I want to be chloroformed and put to bed for a fortnight.'

The chargeless particle was named the neutron. It was at once clear that it must be a constituent of all atomic nuclei (apart from the single-proton nucleus of hydrogen). At last there was an explanation for the puzzle about atomic weights and atomic numbers. The relative weights of atoms are usually near whole numbers: the carbon atom is twelve times as heavy as the hydrogen atom, so its atomic weight is 12. Since electrons are very light, this means that the carbon nucleus is twelve times as heavy as the hydrogen nucleus which consists of a single proton. So the carbon nucleus is as heavy as twelve protons.

Francis Aston and James Chadwick (right) in the mid 1930s. Chadwick's discovery of the neutron explained the puzzle of atomic weights and numbers and solved the problem of isotopes

Opposite: What happens when an atom is split. The series shows the light metal lithium splitting when bombarded by artificially accelerated deuterons, obtained from 'heavy water'. The experiment was first performed by Cockcroft in 1932

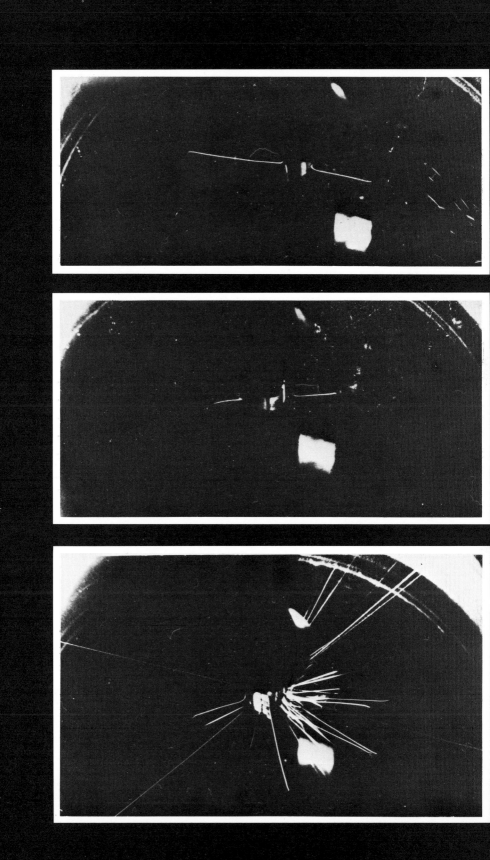

Chemists, however, rank the elements by atomic number, the number of electrons an atom has. It is the electrons which govern an atom's chemical behaviour. But each negatively charged electron 'in orbit' must be balanced by a positively charged proton in the nucleus. The atomic number thus automatically turns out to equal the number of protons in the nucleus. Carbon has an atomic number of 6, it has six protons in the nucleus. With the discovery of the neutron, it became obvious that the difference between its atomic weight of 12 and its atomic number of 6 was made up by six neutrons in the nucleus. They added the mass of six protons to the nucleus without adding any electric charge.

The existence of the neutron also solved at a stroke the problem of isotopes – atoms of the same chemical element, but with different atomic weights. Among a hundred carbon atoms taken at random, ninety-nine have an atomic weight of 12, one is slightly heavier, at 13. Scientists call these isotopes carbon-12 and carbon-13 respectively. Since they have the same chemical properties, each must have six electrons, and a corresponding six protons in the nucleus. The difference in weight must depend on neutrons. Carbon-12 has six neutrons, carbon-13 has seven.

Although the number of neutrons doesn't affect an atom's chemical properties, it – not surprisingly – does change the stability of the nucleus itself. You can add another neutron to carbon-13, to produce carbon-14, with eight neutrons to the six protons. This is too unbalanced. The nucleus is unstable. One of the neutrons spontaneously changes to a proton, emitting a high-speed electron in the process. This radioactive form of carbon is in fact most useful to archaeologists; the gradual decay of carbon-14 atoms enables them to calculate the age of organic remains. The radioactive properties of the different isotopes of the uranium atom were at the end of the decade to have a far more lethal significance.

To return to 1932, though, it was clear that atomic nuclei must have a structure of their own – that is, they were complex entities, with a quite different complexity from the exterior electronic structure of the atom. There was no theory for this nuclear structure, but Bohr's deep imagination was getting to its speculative work. It was too early, and there wasn't enough quantitative detail, for any mathematical expression: but maybe one could begin to guess at primitive models.

In that same year, 1932, atomic nuclei were, for the first time, split under man's direct control. Rutherford and Chadwick had earlier split up nuclei by firing at them the fast alpha particles which naturally shoot out from radium. Now it was feasible to do it all artificially. The projectiles were protons, taken from ordinary hydrogen gas, and accelerated up to enormous speeds by electric fields. This was a process invented and developed by John Cockcroft: it was the beginning of Big Physics, and was to characterize particle physics in years to come – though the Cockcroft accelerator is tiny by the side of the gigantic feats of engineering of which it was the forerunner. The essential thing was, Cockcroft's accelerator worked. Lithium nuclei were duly broken up by his accelerated protons. In about the only magniloquent gesture of a singularly modest and self-effacing life, Cockcroft walked with soft-footed games player's tread through the streets of Cambridge and announced to strangers, 'We've split the atom. We've split the atom.'

It was still a scientific achievement, nothing else but that. The discovery of the neutron had come out of intuition, pure scientific thinking, and experiment. A year later, another particle was discovered, this time not predicted so much as already inscribed in quantum theory. Out of Dirac's equations, it appeared that there must be a positive electron, identical with the familiar electron but carrying the opposite charge. There was a symmetry inherent in the natural world. The positive electron was soon identified in experimental fact, almost simultaneously but quite independently by different types of observation in America and England. Carl D. Anderson got in first, and with justice had the priority. In England Patrick Blackett's publication was a short head behind.

The pressure of sensational results increased. In spite of the gathering political darkness, and the suffering of Jewish scientists in Germany, physics went on still remarkably undisturbed. The next year in Paris, the Joliot-Curies assuaged their chagrin over not recognizing the neutron by producing artificial radioactivity. By bombarding ordinary, stable isotopes of common elements with alpha particles they created new isotopes unknown in nature, and so unstable that they spontaneously broke up and emitted radiation just like the naturally occurring radioactive atoms.

In Rome Fermi and his school carried that major discovery a decisive step further in 1934. To make isotopes with an unusual number of neutrons, they simply bombarded atoms with neutrons, in the hope that they would stick when they hit the target nucleus. Fermi decided to slow the neutrons down by sending them through paraffin. One of his gifts was inspired common sense, and he explained that the neutrons were more likely to stick in the nucleus they were hitting, the slower they moved. Though no one knew it, that apparently prosaic concept was going to have consequences far from prosaic.

At that period, in the early 1930s, no one, and certainly none of the great physicists, had any notion of releasing the energies of the nucleus. It was possible, it had now been done frequently, to split the lightest nuclei. But everyone realized that the forces binding the more complex nuclei were of enormous strength. By bombarding these heavy nuclei, small bits could

Dr E. T. S. Walton, Lord Rutherford, Dr J. D. Cockcroft. Cockcroft and Walton were the first to split the atom by controlled means

be knocked out: but to do more than that, to disintegrate a heavy nucleus and so trigger off what must be gigantic sources of energy, seemed beyond the realms of possibility.

Those leaders of physics were far-sighted men. They were unusually positive in their view. They said as much. In a public lecture in 1933 Rutherford explained that this wonderful crescendo of discovery was getting nearer to the innermost secrets of nature, but that the world was not to expect practical application, nothing like a new source of energy –

such as had once upon a time been hoped for from the forces in the atom. Now we had learned more, and it appeared to be beyond scientific capabilities. Bohr completely agreed. So did Einstein. It is hard to think of three wiser men being so much at one.

Later, in 1934, Fermi bombarded uranium atoms with his slow neutrons. The results were puzzling. The nuclear scientists couldn't agree on an explanation. An abnormal amount of radiation was being emitted. The natural interpretation was that some uranium nuclei had been collecting neutrons, and had been transmuted into elements unknown to nature – christened trans-uranic elements, for they would have heavier nuclei than uranium, the heaviest naturally present on earth. And these very heavy nuclei should be unstable: their radioactive breakdown could produce the copious radiation that Fermi was picking up. The achievement of new, artificial elements – a misinterpretation as it finally transpired – was actually announced in the Italian press with joyous fanfares. What should the new element or elements be called? Fermi, as usual cool-headed, remained somewhat sceptical about his own discovery, but began to believe in it. So did others. There were more random suggestions than had so far happened in any nuclear research. It was a pity, people thought later, that Rutherford, who had died shortly before, wasn't on the scene. It was just the sort of problem that he might have seen straight through.

One of the best chemists in the world, Otto Hahn, decided to repeat the Fermi experiments at the Kaiser Wilhelm Institute in Berlin. Not surprisingly, since Fermi and his colleagues were first-class experimentors, Hahn obtained the same results. Hahn did some careful chemistry on the end-products. The common isotope of uranium, uranium-238, has 92 protons and 146 neutrons in its nucleus. Trans-uranic elements would contain more of both, and have new chemical properties. But what Hahn was expecting to find was radium, on the rival interpretation that the neutrons were simply knocking fragments out of the uranium atom. A uranium atom that loses two alpha particles becomes radium-230.

But he found neither. To his own astonishment, and everyone else's, what he did keep on finding was barium. And barium has a very much lighter nucleus. The common isotope has 56 protons and 82 neutrons; a total of 138 particles bound together in the nucleus, as compared to uranium's 238. And all he could detect was barium. An impurity? But Hahn was one of the most meticulous of all chemists, and that was about as likely as if he had absent-mindedly slipped in some copper sulphate.

Once more suggestions proliferated, much talk, speculations getting nowhere.

When Hahn began to repeat the Fermi work, he had a collaborator called Lise Meitner. Lise Meitner was a respected and much loved physicist on the staff of the Kaiser Wilhelm Institute. She was Jewish, but of Austrian nationality and so, by some skilful covering up, had managed to keep her job. Then Hitler's troops marched into Austria; overnight Lise Meitner's nationality changed to German, and it was more than time to quit. Having good fortune, she managed to escape to Sweden, and it was there, in Göteborg, that she entertained her nephew, Otto Frisch, during the Christmas of 1938. Frisch was another high-class physicist and another refugee who had found sanctuary in Copenhagen. He arrived in Göteborg late at night, and didn't see his aunt until the following morning.

They were an affectionate couple. Both were suffering exile and hardship. Still, the first thing they talked about was her latest letter from Hahn. Why could he detect nothing but barium? Frisch raised the conventional doubts: impurities? carelessness? Impatiently Lise Meitner brushed them aside. She had complete trust in her old chief.

They went for a walk in the winter woods. Each seems to have had the same thought, up to now inadmissible. Like everyone else, they had been living with an assumption. They had all taken it for granted that heavy nuclei couldn't be split into two. Could that be wrong?

Nuclei seemed to be stable objects. Although the positively charged protons must repel one another, as all 'like' electric charges do, the presence of the neutrons glues the nucleus firmly together. Scientists had come to accept that there must be a nuclear force, in addition to the two forces then known – of gravitation and electromagnetism. In the big nuclei, the protons are repelling one another so strongly that there must be more neutrons than protons to keep the whole lot glued together. Even so, some nuclei of the really heavyweight kind – like radium – can't contain all that electric force. Small fragments spontaneously break off. These consist of two protons and two neutrons – a bullet carrying off two units of electric charge and leaving the nucleus more stable. These bullets are the alpha particles, which Rutherford had harnessed to such good effect.

So even when nuclei were unstable, all experience showed that they didn't break up. They simply emitted small fragments. Like all other physicists of the 1930s, Frisch and Meitner were carrying that assumption

Above: Lise Meitner and Otto Hahn in their laboratory, 1920.
Below: The table at which Hahn split the uranium atom when repeating Fermi's experiment in December 1938

with them unquestioned. Now they alone, of all the physicists in the world, woke up to that assumption, and began to question it.

They sat down. It wasn't comfortable in a Swedish Christmas time, but neither noticed that. Lise Meitner did some calculations. Although the structure of the nucleus was still a mystery, Bohr had proposed a model for it. With his great physical insight, Bohr had ignored all the complications – that nothing was known of the nature of nuclear force, for example. Two decades earlier his brilliantly simple model for the electrons in the hydrogen atom had paved the way for the correct, highly sophisticated quantum mechanical answer. Now he simply likened the nucleus to a drop of water. A water drop is held together by the attraction of the water molecules for each other; a nucleus is held together by the nuclear force between its constituents. The analogy is there. Let us not worry about the nature of the nuclear force. The electrical repulsion between the protons could be simply fitted to this model too.

Meitner carried on calculating, using Bohr's liquid-drop model as her guide. Frisch followed her. In Bohr's model the sums were quite simple. Almost at once they knew they had the answer. A heavy nucleus can indeed break into two halves. Imagine a water drop which is electrically charged to the limit of its extent to hold the charge. Water molecules can evaporate from the surface and carry off the excess charge – this is the equivalent of alpha-particle ejection from radium. Alternatively, the stresses within the drop can split it into two smaller drops. These are more tightly bound than larger drops. In the case of nuclei, the two small nuclei can contain the electric charges that made the parent nucleus unstable.

The neutrons that Fermi, and later Hahn, had fired at uranium nuclei had pushed them over the brink. The uranium nuclei didn't accept the neutrons, to build up heavier, trans-uranic, elements. The neutrons didn't just knock off small fragments. Under neutron bombardment, the uranium nuclei split into two smaller, lighter nuclei. The split need not be exactly half and half. A typical break-up would produce barium (with 56 protons) and the gas krypton (which has 36 protons). Here was the reason for Hahn's strange discovery.

Frisch and Meitner did more sums, to check the release of energy. Those came out right. They had been out in the snow for three hours.

They were cautious, as they had to be. The result, in terms of pure science, was important but not earthshaking. Heavy nuclei could be disintegrated. It was going to deepen understanding of the nucleus. They

Lise Meitner arriving in America

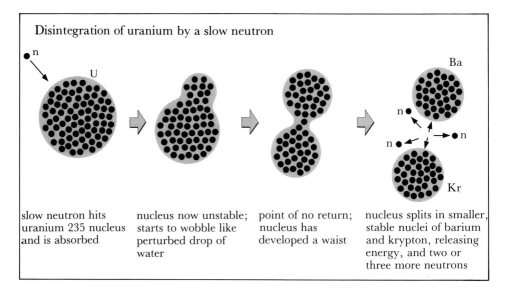

Disintegration of uranium by a slow neutron

| slow neutron hits uranium 235 nucleus and is absorbed | nucleus now unstable; starts to wobble like perturbed drop of water | point of no return; nucleus has developed a waist | nucleus splits in smaller, stable nuclei of barium and krypton, releasing energy, and two or three more neutrons |

had an intimation, though, that the result, in terms other than the purely scientific, might be momentous.

Lise Meitner went back to Stockholm after one of the more remarkable aunt-nephew reunions. Frisch returned to Copenhagen and reported to Bohr. Frisch, not usually an excitable young man, burst into the scientific explanation. Bohr, just about to take a trip to America, accepted the explanation within moments of Frisch beginning to speak. It was then that Bohr made his supreme comment: 'Oh, what idiots we all have been. This is just as it must be.'

It shows the power of a received idea that so many of the best scientific minds in the world had scrabbled about for months, averting themselves from the simplest conclusion. However, they soon made up for lost time. By a loose tongue within Bohr's entourage, the news was leaked as soon as his party arrived in New York. American laboratories repeated the experiment, confirming the results, measuring the energy discharge. Bohr was obliged to ensure that the prime credit went to Meitner-Frisch (whose letter to the science journal *Nature* wasn't, in fact, the first published statement). With his incorruptible sense of justice, he exerted himself in getting the record straight, while he had more imperative matters to think about.

Physicists all over the world were in a ferment. Experiments everywhere. Gossip in newspapers. There were sceptics, but most scientists of

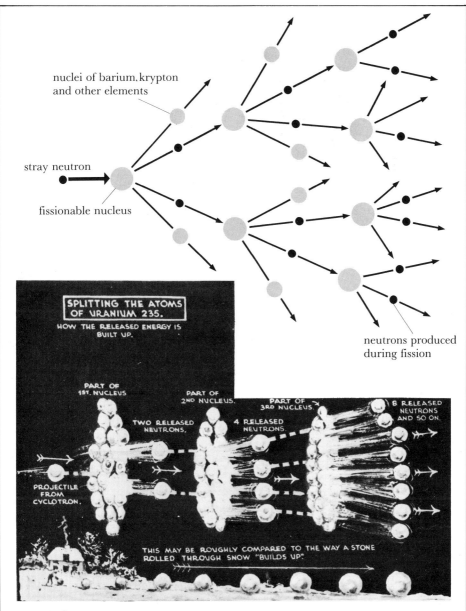

Nuclear chain reaction. The reaction is self-sustaining if at least one neutron from each fission event on the average induces another fission event. If more than one neutron per fission on the average induces another fission, the reaction is explosive. The artist's impression is from a feature in *The Illustrated London News* of 18 August 1945

Scientists of the Crocker Radiation Laboratory at the University of California pose beneath the magnet of Ernest Lawrence's giant atom-smashing cyclotron in 1938. Back row (left to right): A. S. Langsdorf, S. J. Simmons, J. G. Hamilton, D. H. Sloan, J. R. Oppenheimer, W. M. Brobeck, R. Cornog, R. R. Wilson, E. Viez, J. J. Livingwood. Middle row: J. Backus, W. B. Mann, P. C. Aebersold, E. M. McMillan, E. M. Lyman, M. D. Kamen, O. C. Kalbfell, W. W. Salisbury. Front row: J. H. Lawrence, R. Serber, F. N. D. Kurie, R. T. Birge, E. O. Lawrence, D. Cooksey, A. H. Sneill, L. W. Alvarez, P. H. Abelson

Opposite above: Early working model of the cyclotron's 'pan', the chamber in which atomic particles are accelerated in a circular magnetic field before being hurled at the nucleus of the target element

Opposite below: The cyclotron under construction at Berkeley in 1938. The magnet still lacks the upper core and pole faces. The frame is 56 feet long, 30 feet high and 184 inches wide

sober judgement accepted that the discovery must mean that nuclear energy might sometime be set at large. The obvious thought was that this might lead to explosives of stupendous power.

Was this realistic? It would be so only if the neutron which split a uranium nucleus could bring about a chain reaction – a scientific term which soon became a common layman's phrase. Each time a uranium nucleus split apart, it released energy as heat. But nuclear energy would never be a reality if one had to keep firing neutrons from some source at the uranium atoms to break them up. If, on the other hand, the uranium atom released neutrons as it split up, then these neutrons could go on and break up other nuclei. The neutrons from these disintegrations would trigger more, producing a chain of reactions that would carry on without outside help, liberating more and more heat, quicker and quicker. So far there was no sign of that. If there had been, Hahn's laboratory, and a good many others, wouldn't have been in a state to report the results: nor would a number of nice comfortable university towns.

Bohr got to work. So did a young colleague of his at Princeton, John Wheeler, a fine and strong-minded scientist who had the distinction of being the only person of Anglo-Saxon descent right at the centre of these first sensations. He and Bohr arrived at the answer with speed and clarity.

Obviously – and fortunately – most of the uranium nuclei were not being split. A small proportion were. These must belong to a particularly susceptible uranium isotope. Nuclear fission – this term for the splitting of a nucleus was just coming into use – happened not in the stable, common nucleus of uranium (uranium-238), but in that of the much rarer isotope uranium-235. Both have 92 protons, but the neutrons number 146 and 143 respectively. Bohr, now feeling his way with certainty among nuclear structures, gave reasons for the nuclei of uranium-235 being fissile. It was a classical piece of scientific thinking. It was absolutely right. At this distance, it jumps to the eye as being right. But it was not immediately accepted. Fermi, who untypically made several misjudgements during this period, didn't believe it. There were weeks of argument. It was March 1939 before the community of physicists were convinced that this uranium isotope could be disintegrated, emit neutrons, and, if accumulated in quantity, might start a chain reaction. Collect enough uranium-235, and there was the chance of an immense explosion.

There the pure science finished.

7
'This will never happen'

9 August 1945. The smoke billowing 20,000 feet over Nagasaki

The pure science had produced the possibility. By the summer of 1939 it was known all over the scientific world.* Publication was open. The German physicists read the Bohr-Wheeler paper and the rest of the literature with, of course, as much realization as the Americans and English. So did Lev Landau in the Soviet Union, who ranked with Kapitsa as leading Russian physicist. There was much troubled thinking.

Sensible people, certainly in Europe, took it for granted that war was coming, probably within months. It was now feasible at least in principle that explosives could be produced of a different order from any so far in human hands. Was this practicable? Could quantities of these fissile elements ever be made? If so, could it happen in the realistic future, that is within the duration of any foreseeable war?

With a few exceptions, scientific opinion was sceptical. There was plenty of commotion in the press, but, among the immediate prospects of war, these fears were dim and abstract. They did not penetrate to politicians anywhere, who were living, naturally enough, in the present moment, which was sufficiently threatening. Some scientists were blandly optimistic. It would take many years, some of them computed, to accumulate even a few grams of uranium-235. No one then knew how much was needed to make a bomb. But the guess was a quantity which was beyond present-day technological powers.

That wasn't a scientific problem. Science had done its job. All the scientific knowledge was there and ready. If it could ever be applied, that would be a matter of engineering, in particular of abnormally difficult chemical engineering. The only way to separate the uranium isotopes from one another on an industrial scale would be to apply techniques similar to those that the chemical industry already used to separate and purify chemical compounds. In fact, if the discoveries of nuclear fission

* See Appendix i for C. P. Snow's editorial in *Discovery* magazine, September 1939.

had taken place in a peaceful world, their future use would probably have been left to the great firms of the chemical industry – Dupont, ICI and so on. As it was, the ultimate production of the atomic bomb – as was also to be true of space travel – was not a scientific triumph, but an engineering one. In both cases, the science had been ready well before. In the event, scientists had to turn themselves into amateur engineers to play any further operational role.

That summer of 1939 a few scientists were apprehensive and far-sighted. In England, George Thomson (son of J. J.) and W. L. Bragg – both Nobel prize winning physicists – were advising the government to acquire the uranium ore in the Belgian Congo, if only as an insurance. In America the three Hungarian refugees, Edward Teller, Eugene Wigner and Leo Szilard, were campaigning for urgent action. All three had been close to the nuclear developments. All three were scientists of high class, and Wigner was already tipped for the Nobel, which he duly got. All three had inside knowledge of German science, and had much respect for it, even though so many of their old colleagues had been driven out. There was plenty of ability left, they knew, to solve the technological problem of a fission bomb, if the problem could be solved at all. The prospect of a fission bomb in Hitler's control meant nothing short of doom.

On this they were agreed, though they were very different men with, on all other topics, very different opinions. Wigner was calm, judicious, ironic, temperate, mildly conservative: his sister was Dirac's wife. Teller was dramatic, passionate, a man of the right (though more complex in his attitudes than popular accounts later suggested). Szilard was a man of the left, so far as he could be classified at all. He had a temperament uncommon anywhere, maybe a little less uncommon among major scientists. He had a powerful ego and invulnerable egocentricity: but he projected the force of that personality outwards, with beneficent intention towards his fellow creatures. In that sense, he had a family resemblance to Einstein on a reduced scale. He also had an unusually daring scientific imagination. In August 1939, while men as wise as Bohr still found it scarcely credible, Szilard didn't doubt that the fission bomb could be made. That being so, it would be made. Incidentally, Szilard was a writer of interesting scientific fiction. He was the most active spirit among the Hungarian trio. It is likely, though, that Teller also believed that the bomb would be made.

What should they do? They were refugees in a foreign country. They were unknown, except in esoteric academic circles. They wanted to get to

Roosevelt and warn him of the dangers. They decided to go to Einstein and persuade him to write a letter. Einstein was himself a refugee – he had been in the United States since 1930 – but he was the opposite of unknown. They duly went out to his summer retreat on Long Island and explained their thoughts. It hasn't been stated, but the conversation must have been mostly in German. Einstein thought that they were completely right. The letter was drafted by Szilard. Einstein signed it.*

Then they indulged in some Central European elaboration. Not knowing how American politics worked, they resorted to finesse. Szilard had discovered someone who appeared to have the entrée to the President, an economist called Alexander Sachs. It would probably have been better to do what a simpler character such as Ernest Lawrence – the American physicist who won the 1939 Nobel prize for his improved particle acceleration – would have done, and use straightforward channels. Anyway, Sachs did deliver the letter to the President, though it took six weeks. Then there was an anticlimax. Nothing happened.

The romantic myth that Einstein was ultimately responsible for the atomic bomb has no foundation. It is true that much later he expressed some guilt about signing the famous letter, but that was taking an unnecessary burden upon his conscience. What is not in doubt is that he felt as strongly as the others that bitter necessity dictated that the bomb should be made. The threat of a Nazi bomb was enough. There were no moral qualms at that stage. Einstein had, for most of his life, been a pacifist. With the advent of Hitler he accepted that he had been wrong. He told old friends, who still clung to sweet optimistic dreams, that they were being foolishly unrealistic. Whatever military force meant, whatever the bomb meant, the anti-Hitler side must have it first.

That was the view, quite unqualified, of all who were not absolute pacifists (of whom in those scientific circles there were very few). It is desirable not to subtilize ethical attitudes after the event. There was no scientist or anyone else involved who didn't believe that the work was necessary. That included Einstein and Bohr, who were among the loftiest and most benign spirits of our species. They don't need to receive moral instruction from persons who did not live inside the situation.

The real impulse which led to the manufacture of the bomb came six months later. It was provided by two more refugees, Rudolf Peierls and Otto Frisch, the latter for the second time playing a decisive part.

* See Appendix ii.

They were working in Oliphant's physics department at Birmingham. With the death of Rutherford, the Cavendish stars had scattered all over Britain. At Birmingham Oliphant's staff provided two of the major scientific contributions to the war. One was the invention by Randall and Boot of the cavity magnetron. This electronic device made it possible to generate intense, short-wavelength radio beams, which made the British radar far better than anything the Germans could achieve. It was the most valuable English scientific innovation in the Hitler war. The other was a paper of three pages, factual, succinct, accurately prophetic, by Peierls and Frisch.

They started with two acute clarifications. First, they accepted wholeheartedly what other physicists had been peculiarly hesitant about, namely the Bohr-Wheeler doctrine: it must be the isotope uranium-235 which had been disintegrated, and nothing else. Second, they were certain, knowing more of the latest chemical engineering than some of their colleagues, that it would be nothing like so difficult as had been generally assumed to separate this isotope from its natural intimate mixture with the far more abundant uranium-238, and produce uranium-235 in a relatively pure form.

From that, all else followed. It would need a certain amount of this isotope to set off cumulative disintegration, that is a chain reaction, which meant a nuclear bomb. They calculated what this amount would have to be, and came up with a startlingly small answer. It would need only about a kilogram (just over two pounds). This was called the critical mass. Smaller masses of uranium-235 are stable; larger amounts are not. To make a bomb, simply bring together two approximately equal parts, half a kilo each. As soon as they touch, the whole mass should explode with a force unequalled in human history. It was surprisingly simple. The reasoning was set down in about a thousand words and a few matter-of-fact calculations. It was convincing to anyone who could read scientific argument. It proved to be in all essentials correct. The estimates of quantities were just about right. The requirements for a fission bomb could be put in a couple of small suitcases. The concept of the bomb had been floating in the air. With those three typewritten pages, the practical manufacture got its first initiative.

It would require an immense industrial development. It was one thing to talk of separating the isotope on this scale, but a formidable job to do it. Britain might just conceivably have been able to try, in peace-time. But the country was at war, and still had to survive: which meant that an abnormal proportion of its resources had to be spent on radar, a device not only sensible but vital, and on bombing aircraft, which was not so sensible.

America was still not in the war. It took some time for the Peierls-Frisch memorandum to reach American scientists. It was carried over the Atlantic in August 1940 by Cockcroft, who talked in his quiet uninflected manner to American nuclear scientists. A good many were working on uranium projects, but there was not the urgency that was driving British scientists, who, in the good old Johnsonian mood, had their minds concentrated by the prospect of being hanged tomorrow. But it didn't take long for the Americans to be convinced that the uranium-235 bomb was feasible.

And American physicists had just discovered another isotope which could be used in a fission bomb. This was not an isotope of uranium. Edwin McMillan, with colleagues Philip Abelson and Glenn Seaborg, had achieved what Fermi thought he had done – they had produced trans-uranic elements. Not surprisingly, these had unstable, radioactive nuclei. The new element beyond uranium was called neptunium – because the planet Neptune is beyond Uranus in the solar system. But it was the next element that was bomb material. Called – inevitably – plutonium, element number 94 has an isotope, plutonium-239, which can sustain a chain reaction of disintegrations. Making a plutonium bomb is not so much a question of separating isotopes, but of making sizeable quantities of an element that does not occur in nature. This, however, need not be any more difficult than separating the uranium isotopes; the plutonium bomb had strong advocates, too.

The Einstein letter hadn't produced much in the way of action. Now the entire US governmental scientific machine began to get to work. American energy was set free in its impressive abundance. The project was codenamed Manhattan. There was, of course, an element of fright communicated by the British. The Peierls-Frisch argument was only too convincing. It now seemed odds on that atomic bombs were makeable. What were the Nazis doing?

The Manhattan project was a feat of technology and scientific administration. As has been said, the essential science had been done earlier. This was application on a gigantic scale. There were, in fact, scientific snags along the way, and plenty of puzzles on the frontiers of science and engineering. A number of the best scientists alive showed considerable versatility in attacking problems utterly different from anything they had met in an academic department. Fermi, who was able to apply his mind to almost anything – on his death-bed he wished that he had given a little thought to politics – was prepared to invent devices of extreme sophistication and occasionally, in an un-American fashion, of childlike simplicity. By common consent, he was the most valuable man around. But many others displayed talents which no one, including themselves, imagined that they possessed. At Los Alamos in New Mexico, which was the brain centre of the project, they lived a life remote but intense, certain that the job was imperative, not worried (such worry is swept away in war) by consequences. It was exciting to be living near a peak of technical achievement.

The chief scientific administrator, Robert Oppenheimer, was one of the most interesting figures in world science. Among a mass of very clever men, he was probably the cleverest. He was highly cultivated in the arts, and had an admirably organized and structured mind. He had genuine scientific talent, and could talk on equal terms with the greatest scientists in the place. Bohr, who was finally evacuated from Denmark via Sweden to London and Los Alamos, at the risk of his life, had a very high opinion of Oppenheimer's scientific gift. So had Rabi, the least soft of touches.

The curious thing was that Oppenheimer had no great scientific achievement to his name. This is hard to explain. He had lived through a period in which men with a tenth of his talent had made major discoveries. He was scientifically ambitious and would have liked real creative success more than anything in the world. He became a great figure: the achievement of Los Alamos made him famous and he deserved the fame. Nevertheless, one suspects he would have given all that away if he could have exchanged it for one single piece of work of the class, say, of Pauli's Exclusion Principle. There was his tragedy, probably much more deeply wounding than the political misfortunes which later happened to him.

There were some other strangenesses about the population of Los Alamos. A high proportion were refugees, recent immigrants who had had time to be rapidly naturalized. This was partly, of course, because they included some of the best practitioners on earth: but there was another reason. Most native scientists, in America and even more in Britain, had been swept up in work which appeared, and was, more directly concerned with the Hitler war. For example, Cockcroft, who would have been peculiarly valuable at Los Alamos, was head of an English radar establishment. (He had to be extracted later to lead the British nuclear team in Canada.) Rabi was immersed in similar activities at the Massachusetts Institute of Technology, and so on for dozens of the top American and English nuclear scientists. Refugees were the main source of the available manpower of high class. This may or may not have made a marginal difference when it came to disputes about the long-term political future of what they were doing. Refugees sometimes felt constrained. They wanted to accept the country which they hoped to make their own.

The dominance of refugees had some more farcical concomitants.

Security procedures were thrown into a frenzy and at times displayed their dottier aspects. For example, Peierls and Frisch were never given places on Maud, the small British committee responsible for work on the nuclear bomb – and so weren't able, in official terms, to discuss and explain *their own work*.

It was Fermi who took the first step into the nuclear age. Although no one now had any doubt that the bomb was possible, it was important to test that chain reactions could take place. Physicists needed to monitor, to

Birth of the Atomic Age, by Gary Sheahan. The cadmium rods are withdrawn and Fermi's graphite-uranium reactor becomes operational, producing the world's first sustained nuclear chain reaction

measure, a nuclear chain reaction that went leisurely. Fermi achieved this with naturally occurring uranium, where the overwhelming amount of stable uranium-238 would prevent an explosion. His earlier intuition that slow neutrons were best at instigating nuclear fission was vital. This time he used blocks of graphite to slow them. In a disused squash court at the University of Chicago he built an edifice from six tons of uranium, fifty tons of uranium oxide and four hundred tons of graphite blocks: he called it a 'pile', because it was literally that. But in present-day terms it was the first nuclear reactor.

On 2 December 1942, Fermi withdrew the neutron-absorbing 'control rods'. The chain reaction began. Neutrons split the minority of uranium-235 nuclei; heat and more neutrons streamed from the disintegration. These neutrons shot out of the uranium block, but were slowed by the graphite, and so split more uranium-235 nuclei as they entered the next uranium block. Fermi's pile was not designed to produce nuclear power as such. It was a test. After making his measurements, Fermi took it apart again. Theoretically, at least, the path to the bomb was now clear.

Scientists at Los Alamos were certainly all confident that it would not be long before a bomb was ready. They had the euphoria of all concerned in an extraordinary enterprise. That was the overmastering emotion. Apprehensions about the putative Nazi performance were lessening slightly – though in official London the word still went round that the war was going well *if we are safe from that which we mustn't talk about.*

It would have horrified General Leslie Groves, the supreme administrator of the Manhattan project, to discover how badly his security system actually worked. It was nothing like so effective as security about the decoding techniques (the English called this process Ultra). Groves's iron rules certainly made communication between the people doing the job at times bizarrely complicated. Another result was to prevent any news of the operation reaching the Vice President of the United States and the Deputy Prime Minister of the United Kingdom: but a good deal of news reached hundreds of other people. This wasn't because of treachery or even gossip. Men like Groves underestimate the intelligence of their fellow citizens. Why were well-known scientists disappearing to unknown destinations? Why should Niels Bohr arrive in London and shortly afterwards get swallowed up in America? To scientists, it was all too obvious.

Niels Bohr was both unusually busy and unusually worried. After inspecting the diffusion plants where the uranium isotopes were

Target holder for a cyclotron built by Fermi. *Above:* The first plutonium compound isolated by man, prepared by Glenn Seaborg's team at Chicago University on 10 September 1942

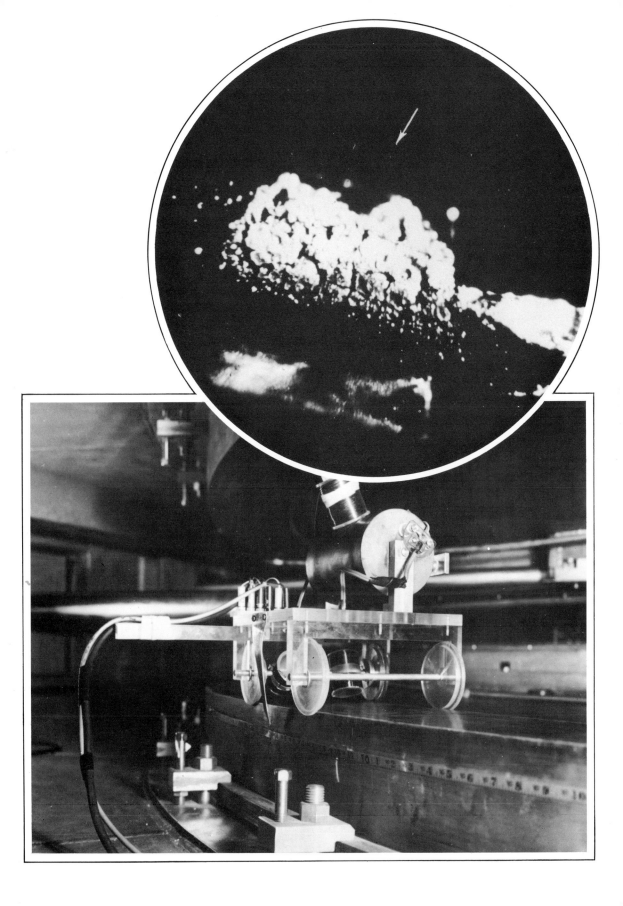

separated, he had no doubt that the nuclear bomb was a certainty: and, what was more, not just a certainty for this war, but a feature of the world scene for ever. He was one of the most far-sighted of men, and he belonged to the world. He went to Los Alamos, anxious to help where he could, but deliberately not attaching himself formally to either the American or British contingents. He knew another certainty. It was taking America about four years to make the bomb: it wouldn't take long for the Soviet Union, or other industrialized societies with a strong enough purpose, to do the same. Nearly all scientists agreed. There are no secrets in science: and very few, and those short-lived, in technology.

From the moment it became known that the Americans were moving towards a fission bomb, the general guess was that it would take the Soviet Union perhaps five years to catch up – some, more in touch with Soviet engineering physics, thought that was an over-estimate. General Groves gave contemptuous snorts. He told his political masters that the United States had at least a twenty-year lead, probably much more. That was believed by those who wanted to believe, and produced some political dangers. General Groves was a singularly bad choice for his job.

Bohr, after characteristic reflection, decided that it was worth trying to avert or minimize the post-war perils which any sentient person could imagine. It would do no harm, and might do some good, to give the Soviet government an indication about the bomb. (We now know they were already informed. Bohr didn't know this, but he assumed that their scientists had made their own predictions from 1939 onwards, as had duly happened.) Even a tentative disclosure, Bohr thought, might make for international confidence.

Bohr revealed his thoughts to Halifax, the British Ambassador in Washington, and received considerable sympathy, as he did from Felix Frankfurter. He was despatched to have a talk, with Churchill.

That encounter was one of the black comedies of the war. For some obscure reason, Churchill was strongly averse to seeing Bohr. It wasn't that he didn't come with the highest recommendations. Sir John Anderson, whom no one could think had pro-Soviet leanings, had already heard Bohr's case, and thought there was a lot in it. It perhaps wasn't irrelevant that Anderson had had a scientific education, had even done some research, and found it easy to believe the temporary nature of the Western lead. He also had great respect for Bohr. So presumably did Cherwell, who couldn't have been well disposed to the actual proposal, but knew all about Bohr and helped force the interview on Churchill. The President of the Royal Society had also insisted. After all, Bohr was one of the greatest men of the century.

After very long and discourteous delays, Bohr was granted a discourteous half hour. It bore a resemblance, seen through a distorting mirror, to the meeting with Rutherford which got Bohr launched on his career. No doubt Bohr whispered conscientiously alone. This time, however, the other party wasn't prepared to listen, or apparently didn't trouble to understand what was being said. On the stroke of the half hour Bohr was dismissed.

Bohr didn't suffer from offended dignity. But he was miserable. He had failed in what he believed to be his most important public mission.

Would Einstein have done better? Probably not, so far as the outcome went. There would have been a difference of tone. Einstein was not outfaced by any man alive, and there would have been some Jehovianic words spoken from his side of the table.

That meeting, if one can use an inappropriate word, took place in the summer of 1944, just before the invasion of Europe. As soon as the Anglo-American forces got a foothold in Germany, a mission was despatched to investigate what the German nuclear physicists had really been doing. The mission consisted of two excellent physicists, both originally Dutch, now American, Goudsmit and Uhlenbeck. Their report was pleasing but surprising. The German nuclear physicists had done remarkably little. As had been thought, Heisenberg had been in charge of a group, small but high-powered. The members were to be interrogated in England as soon as they could be tracked down. Anyway, that specific war-long anxiety was now wiped away.

So only the Americans, with their British affiliates, had been making the bomb. Bohr, nothing if not pertinacious, continued with his resolve. Brushed off by Churchill, he went back to American confidants, Frankfurter, Vannevar Bush (the first of presidential scientific advisers), J. B. Conant. They, too, had been trying to read the future, and were ready to support Bohr. It was arranged for him to explain his thoughts to Roosevelt.

There he got a very different response from Churchill's. It was warm, cordial, amiably sympathetic. With knowledge of what followed within three months, this now seems puzzling. It may have been just a politician's professional technique, but it appears more likely that the President

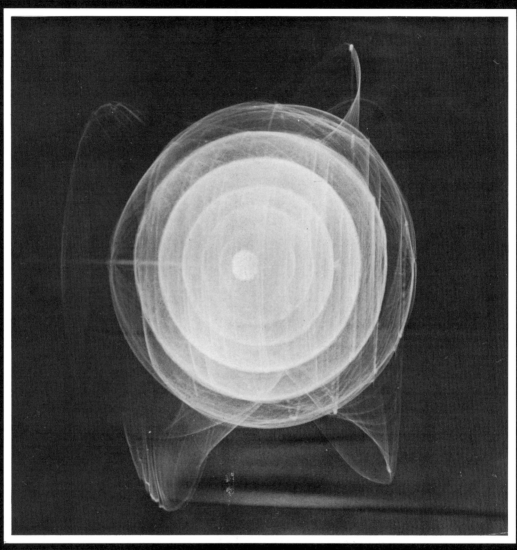

Model of the uranium atom in motion. British exhibit at the Atoms for
Peace Conference, Geneva, 1955

was at least half impressed. He would, of course, have been carefully briefed by Bush and the others, and he had picked up more about Bohr himself than Churchill had. Churchill seems to have taken a violent personal dislike to Bohr – about the only human being who ever did so.

It would be false to give the impression that the scientists at Los Alamos had any knowledge of these attempts to cope with the future. Bohr was much too punctilious and honourable to let slip any word of those discussions, though two or three of his senior colleagues, Fermi and Oppenheimer among them, had an intimation of what was being tried and agreed with it, though without much hope. Most of the Los Alamos population wouldn't have felt it as a personal concern. They knew that the project was soon going to succeed or fail. Failure was unthinkable, and yet some couldn't suppress the thought as the gigantic enterprise approached its climax.

The Manhattan project was now employing 500,000 people, directly and indirectly, and spending a billion dollars per year. The uranium isotopes were separated by two different processes – at the beginning, no one knew which would be the more efficient. The first was a diffusion process. When the metal uranium reacts with fluorine, the compound formed – uranium hexafluoride – is a gas. A molecule containing uranium-238 is very slightly heavier than a molecule of uranium-235 hexafluoride, and as a result is slightly more sluggish. If uranium hexafluoride gas made from natural uranium – which contains only 0.7 per cent uranium-235 – is forced through a filter, the lighter uranium-235 will find it slightly easier to get through. So the gas on the far side is marginally enriched in the required isotope. Repeat the process, and the proportion of uranium-235 will rise a little more. To get 'weapons-grade' uranium – containing 90 per cent of the rare isotope – needed thousands of passes through the filters. But, slow though it was, it was gradually accumulating the fissile material.

Running in parallel was separation by means of electric and magnetic fields. Uranium atoms were stripped of electrons in a vacuum. Now they were electrically charged, and they were susceptible to outside fields. Again the heavier uranium-238 was more sluggish, and uranium-235 could gradually be separated out.

And plutonium was now in 'commercial scale' production – kilograms of a new element were being created. In huge reactors, uranium was bombarded by neutrons. The important isotope this time was the common uranium-238, which absorbed a neutron, then emitted two electrons from the nucleus and ended up as plutonium-239. With large quantities of plutonium to investigate, the scientists had found that it was indeed fissile – something they had had to take on trust from the theoreticians at the beginning of the Manhattan project.

The bomb, or more exactly one uranium bomb and one plutonium bomb, should be ready by the late summer of 1945, a year ahead. There would be a test just before the bombs were despatched.

Thus very few at Los Alamos had any glimmer of the first results of Bohr's diplomacy. This was another piece of black comedy. Roosevelt and Churchill met at the second Quebec conference. Roosevelt surrendered without a struggle to Churchill's view of Bohr. He was on the verge of 'mortal crimes' – an extraordinary Churchillian phrase. Churchill drew up his and Roosevelt's understanding. Nothing whatever about the project was to be communicated to anyone outside the circle of secrecy, certainly not to the French, above all not to the Russians. Bohr, and anyone under his influence, was to be kept under surveillance.

At one point Churchill was demanding that Bohr should be arrested. That was, however, too much for the President's advisers and Churchill's own, many of them shaken by this singular display. Possibly the only person who wasn't shaken was Admiral Leahy, who, with his habitual lack of judgement, was certain that the bomb would be a fiasco and wouldn't go off at all.

Why did Roosevelt and Churchill behave like that? Roosevelt was a sick man, and may not have felt capable of resisting Churchill in one of his obsessive nagging phases, prepared to go on grinding away in perpetuity. But Churchill? There has never been much of an explanation. He had always had a naive faith in 'secrets'. He had been told by the best authorities that this 'secret' wasn't keepable and that the Soviets would soon have the bomb themselves. Perhaps, with one of his surges of romantic optimism, he deluded himself into not believing it. He was only too conscious that British power, and his own, was now just a vestige. So long as the Americans and British had the bomb in sole possession, he could feel that that power hadn't altogether slipped away.

It is a sad story. Probably the result didn't make any real difference. Even if Bohr had prevailed, and there had been some attempt at international understanding, in practical terms everything would have gone on as it actually did in America, the Soviet Union, the United Kingdom,

France, and in due course a good many other countries. There might have been a faint improvement in external civility, which is sometimes worth having. But the story remains a sad one, and something of a symbol.

Meanwhile the manufacture of the first bomb went on, the pace of sheer activity increasing. The Hitler war ended but there was no let-up. It was an illusion believed by many that there was a whole arsenal of bombs. That wasn't true for a long time. There was an assembly on a tower, not an actual bomb, for the test – a plutonium device. Two bombs (one of each) which should be ready for use; one more plutonium bomb was in reserve. The rest consisted of threats.

By this time none of the scientists had doubts that the bomb would work: or at least no such doubt appeared in records or memoirs. Some political placemen, like the ineffable Leahy, added to their reputation for hardbitten wisdom by continuing to regard the whole project as nonsense, a kind of longhaired hoax that wouldn't produce anything more lethal than a popgun.

Some of the scientists, though, had a different worry. They were sure that the bombs would be ready for use: but what would they be used for? Not many people seemed to have answered the question. The bombs had been made as an insurance against the Nazis making them too and they hadn't needed to think further than that. Now the Nazis were eliminated. A whisper spread that the American military were intending to use the bombs on Japan.

Some of the American scientists had relatives in the forces who would be fighting if there was an invasion of Japan. For them the ethical problem was simple: anything to get that war over. Just as the most charitable of Russians years later used to say, not lightly, that if they had possessed the bomb in early 1945, they would have dropped it on Berlin. They had lost too many men to have qualms. But most of the scientists were free to have such qualms. They hadn't access to diplomatic intelligence, which would have increased their misgivings. Still, it was enough to know that here was the climactic feat of applied science: it just couldn't be used for mass extermination without a thought. At the very least, there must be a demonstration. Warn the Japanese, drop a bomb in the sea. That would tell its own story. After that, consciences would be relatively clean.

Something like that was in fact proposed by Josef Franck, the leader of the Chicago group, another Nobel prize winner, a refugee from Göttingen and, like Born, another witness to the old German culture. He and half a

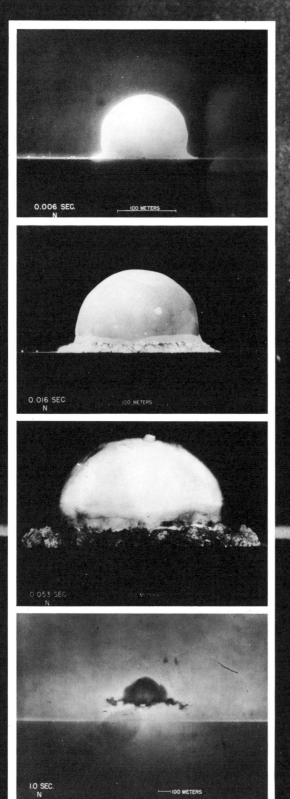

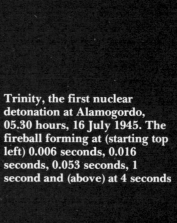

Trinity, the first nuclear
detonation at Alamogordo,
05.30 hours, 16 July 1945. The
fireball forming at (starting top
left) 0.006 seconds, 0.016
seconds, 0.053 seconds, 1
second and (above) at 4 seconds

Above: Oppenheimer and General Groves at the Trinity test site after the explosion

Uranium bomb of the 'Little Boy' type dropped on Hiroshima. The bomb was 28 inches in diameter and 120 inches long. It weighed 9000 lbs and had a yield equivalent to 20,000 tons of high explosive

dozen of his colleagues sent a statement to Washington. It had one vestige of a result. A small group of the Manhattan scientists were asked to give their opinion. This group consisted of Oppenheimer, Fermi, Ernest Lawrence, and the British Nobel prize winner A. H. Compton. They replied within a matter of days. Their opinions divided down the middle, two on each side. Oppenheimer and Fermi were in favour of dropping the bomb (actually the two bombs) without any preliminaries. Lawrence and Compton were against.

Probably nothing, or no representations from any man alive, could have stopped the bomb being used. As Einstein was to remark years later, there was a weird inevitability about it all.

The events that followed in July and August 1945 have often been described. The test at Alamogordo in the New Mexico desert went exactly according to expectation. If anything, the explosion was more powerful than predicted. It was one thing to have expectations, to believe in the certainties of reason: it was even more satisfactory to see them fulfilled as the most brilliant exhibition created by man. The scientists were jubilant, and they wouldn't have been human if they hadn't been. Fermi, with one of his Heath Robinson contrivances, was measuring blast by means of tin cans and pieces of paper. Someone more sardonic than the rest remarked that it was the most expensive dry run in scientific history.

The bombs were duly dropped. On 6 August Hiroshima was the target for the uranium-235 bomb; Nagasaki suffered the plutonium bomb three days later. Why was the second judged necessary? The question elicited comments, some cynical, some heart-wrung. There were utterances, in public and private, all over the physicists' world. The scientists have learned sin, said Oppenheimer. That was too rhetorical for what they truly felt. Many of them were searching for some effective action. Mark Oliphant not only made his speech about the death of a beautiful subject, but also was demanding that England and his own Australia should make the bomb themselves. Any country without it was helpless from now on. Others were campaigning for international control, as Bohr had urged on Churchill in their grotesque meeting.

However, those thoughts of August 1945 weren't to survive for very long. The future was to become not quite so apocalyptic. Physics hadn't been killed, and the beautiful subject stayed beautiful, though in forms as yet unimaginable. While applied physics, and the technology born out of it, was not to have ended with the bomb, but scarcely to have begun.

8
Nuclear fusion

8156B1945 or The Hiroshima Cartoon, a painting by Graham Ashton

When the news of Hiroshima was first broadcast, a select assembly of German nuclear scientists (Heisenberg and Hahn amongst them) were in gentlemanly captivity in a Cambridgeshire country house. Their conversation was bugged. To begin with, they didn't believe the BBC report. This wasn't a fission bomb. It was some kind of bluff, designed to frighten the Japanese into making peace. After all, they, the Germans, hadn't found a way of making such a bomb. How could the Anglo-Americans have done so?

The mystery was the exact opposite. Why hadn't the Germans come nearer? The answer seems to be that, until late in the war, the German authorities, with whom decisions usually went much too high, often to Hitler himself, weren't prepared to devote resources to projects which wouldn't guarantee results within a couple of years. They wanted weapons for use next year, not in the dim future. Their engineering was still excellent, in many fields much better than that of the Anglo-Americans. They were producing the jet fighter, Me 262, by far the best fighter in the war, which didn't come into service until too late. Similarly with their final type of submarine. But they didn't expend any of that engineering skill on a nuclear bomb. That was too remote, and might as well be left to the scientists.

The scientists appear not to have had much access to high authority, or not much influence. Further, good as they were, as good as their counterparts in America, they didn't show themselves as flexible and adaptable. Apparently, though it seems inexplicable, they had no equivalent of the Peierls-Frisch calculations about the practicality of the bomb (the Germans were thinking in terms much more gigantesque). The German scientists didn't transform themselves into wartime engineers. They had no Fermi. If they had acquired him, it could have made a difference.

There gradually emerged a sweet romantic story, much to the credit of human nature, that the German scientists had deliberately held back.

They wouldn't accept the moral responsibility of giving such bombs to a monstrous regime. It would be an intolerable crime. Better to pretend that the bomb wasn't feasible.

Well, it is a sweet story, but it happens to be utterly untrue. These were decent men: they were also dutiful men and, some of them, nationalistic Germans. Heisenberg had visited Bohr in occupied Copenhagen in 1941, and Bohr was certain that it was an attempt, not to inquire if Allied scientists had conscientious scruples, but whether they were setting about the job. From 1943 onwards, men as intelligent as Heisenberg knew that their country was fighting a desperate defensive war. If they lost, that was the end of Germany. Even under Nazi rule, Germany was Germany. In comparable circumstances, American, English, Russian scientists would have felt that the evils of the regime counted for nothing against the evils of absolute defeat. They would have gone to the limit to make the bomb.

Nothing is known in the West of whether the Soviets had started their own nuclear project before the end of the war. As with the Germans, they were fighting a desperate war, and may not have been able to spare effort for longer-term enterprises. They certainly knew a good deal about what was happening in America. They had their legitimate sources of intelligence: and others, such as Klaus Fuchs, not so legitimate. When Stalin was told at Potsdam that the bomb was ready, it can't have come as a surprise.

Whether they had started before or not, they threw immense energy into catching up. The only genuine secret, as someone said, was that the bomb had been made. It wasn't hard, as Bohr and others had tried to impress upon the politicians years before, for another technological society to make it. Politicians, or some of them, still listened to General Groves and similar thinkers – it would take a generation for the Soviets to possess their own bomb. It took four years. That figure had been about the average of the scientists' estimates.

The nuclear arms race was on. There was a sudden acceleration which made many thoughtful men lose what remained of their wits. It became likely that a different kind of nuclear bomb, many times more powerful than the fission bomb, could be developed. This was the hydrogen, or fusion, bomb.

In the Hiroshima and Nagasaki bombs, the heaviest of atomic nuclei – uranium and plutonium – broke up into smaller, more stable nuclei. The most stable of all nuclei, in fact, are intermediate-weight ones, like iron,

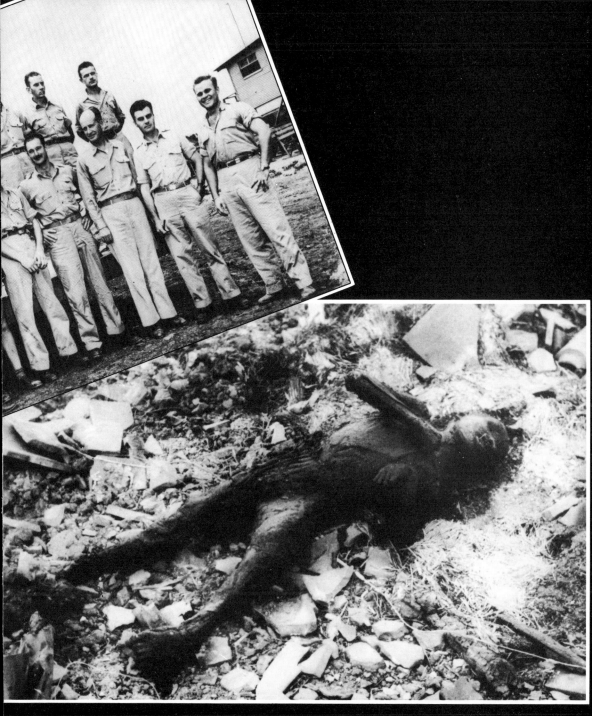

Above: Hiroshima victim

Opposite: The mushroom cloud over Hiroshima seen from the US Air Force plane, Enola Gay, moments after the bomb was dropped on 6 August 1945

Centre: Snapshot of the crew of the Enola Gay taken at the air base on the Pacific island of Tinian. Only two members knew the mission's secret

Huge crowds gather in Times Square to celebrate
America's victory over Japan

which has 56 nuclear particles (26 protons and 30 neutrons). This means that one can take a different route to nuclear energy: join together – 'fuse' – the very lightest elements of all to make slightly heavier nuclei, and thereby generate energy. Before the war, astrophysicists had calculated that the sun – and most other stars – makes energy this way. At the sun's core, hydrogen nuclei (protons) get together in fours to make helium nuclei. The energy liberated is sunshine.

But it is also possible to release the energy of hydrogen fusion explosively, and it is far more efficient than the fission of uranium or plutonium. Should a hydrogen bomb be made, it would be a thousand times more powerful than the fission bomb. Such a bomb could annihilate the largest of cities, London, Chicago, Moscow. It would be the ultimate weapon.

Could it be made? Should it be made?

About the answer to the first question, most of the leaders hadn't much doubt. The history of the fission bomb had made them technologically confident. What was possible in theory, had proved to be workable in practice. At first inspection, there didn't look to be quite the number of critical problems that they had had to grapple with between 1941 and 1945. (In actual fact, there turned out to be some of extreme difficulty.)

As for the second question – should the bomb be made? – everyone knew what the answer was going to be. This was a weapon of war, different in kind, more lethal by a thousand times than any in existence. Has any advance, even a tiny one, in a weapon of war ever been abnegated in the whole of human history? Because of the demands of human conscience, that is. Many such advances have been missed because of miscalculation or stupidity, but that is a somewhat less interesting matter.

Still, though the issue was a foregone conclusion, there were scruples, doubts, hesitations, such as there hadn't been about the first nuclear bomb. Then – so it had seemed – it could mean immediate life or death. This time the dangers were harder to foresee and in any case were much longer-term. Oppenheimer was in a state of moral anxiety. He lived closer to his own experience than most decision-makers, and he was in contact with what others thought about him and what he thought about himself. He would have liked a good reason, technical or military, why the hydrogen bomb shouldn't be proceeded with. He didn't find one. He was for once unable to explain his doubts with precision. Previously, though he was too sensitive for an ideal man of action, he had been able to command his own will. Now, it seems that he couldn't.

Einstein and Oppenheimer at Princeton in 1949. Both men were deeply
opposed to the development of the H-bomb

In Moscow there was a dilemma which had some family resemblances. Kapitsa decided that he could not work on the hydrogen bomb. The American and Soviet discussions and plans were proceeding almost simultaneously. Kapitsa's reasons for wanting to contract out were not the same as Oppenheimer's. Kapitsa was a civilized and enlightened man, a descendant of the professional (not landed) Russian upper class, for so long in Tsarist times the guardians of liberal hopes. His father and paternal grandfather had both been distinguished generals in the Tsarist army, but that didn't prevent them sharing those hopes. On the other hand, a military family, however enlightened, is impelled to put the safety of the country first and foremost. Certainly Stalin thought so, and never, and rightly, had any suspicions about Kapitsa's fundamental loyalty – which was fortunate for the hundred or more scientists, mainly Jewish, whom Kapitsa saved in the worst days of the purges, from 1937 to 1940, which Russians call the *Yezhovshchina*. Kapitsa took many risks, but, as he'd had with Rutherford, he could have some influence with Stalin. He was later known to say that those two were the only men who ever loved him.

It is unlikely that Kapitsa's main motive in refusing to collaborate on the hydrogen bomb was, in the narrow sense, humanitarian. He was a much tougher-minded man than Oppenheimer, and it is far more probable that he would have argued that if one superpower possessed this super-bomb, the other had better have it too. He always had a deep, almost sensual, Russian patriotism. It would be wrong, perhaps, to eliminate all thoughts of revulsion at mass slaughter on a world scale brought about by scientific means. A good many scientists felt that revulsion, at the time, and since. Kapitsa seems, however, to have had a more professional reason for absenting himself. His institute, he himself, would be important figures in the H-bomb programme. The officials – presumably the technical officers at the Ministry of Defence – proposed to tell him what to do. That he couldn't and wouldn't take. He knew that on this kind of job he was as valuable as any man in the Soviet Union. He wanted his own way.

He remained obdurate. All that happened to him was a mild form of house-arrest. Since his house was a hundred yards across a kind of college court from his own institute, that didn't cut him off from his own research. Scientific publications flowed in as usual. He brooded in a classical Russian fashion. As soon as the house-arrest was called off, all acted as though it hadn't been. He received a Nobel prize twenty years later, in his eighties.

Large teams in the United States and the Soviet Union busied themselves with the hydrogen bomb. Some of the participants in the fission bomb programme were in this project also, such as the still young John Wheeler. Not much is known of the Soviet scientists actively involved, with one exception.

In both countries two men who became, in rather different ways, world figures, had commanding responsibility for the hydrogen bomb. Both had great technical (scientific and technological) daring and exceptionally strong wills. In America Edward Teller, in the popular view, later became the chief scientific spokesman of the conservative right, and was known, rather more justly, as the father of the H-bomb. In the Soviet Union a much younger man, still in his twenties when he achieved his major work, fulfilled something close to the same function. The details are not yet known, but his achievement may have been similar to Teller's. The young man was Andrei Sakharov, whom more worldly Russians described as a pure soul rather like Dirac, and who in middle age spoke in Moscow as the most intellectually creditable of dissidents.

It doesn't need saying that the H-bomb was duly made. From start to finish, it took the American scientists just under four years and the Soviet scientists a few months longer. Once again, this was something like what cool-minded observers had reckoned on.

The H-bomb was the last dramatic contribution of high science to the world's military situation. In the 1950s it brought a sense of doom to many men of good sense and good will. It did so to Einstein, who died in 1956. He spent some of his final energies warning humanity about its dangers. He didn't do that sentimentally, for, as has been said, he was the least sentimental of men. His heart does not bleed, his eyes do not weep, said someone who idolized him. He took it as a final duty, having ceased to expect much sensible behaviour from humankind. He faced his own death with majestic and impersonal composure, saying that on this earth he had done his job. Few men could have said that with more justification.

There was one job, however, that he hadn't finished. He hadn't discovered the 'unified field theory', the search for which had occupied the second half of his life.

After his brilliant explanation of gravitation in his General Theory of Relativity back in 1915, Einstein had spent the rest of his life in an attempt

Andrei Sakharov, father of Russia's H-bomb. The postcard,
smuggled out of the USSR, shows that despite his
banishment Sakharov is still in touch with current research
in theoretical physics

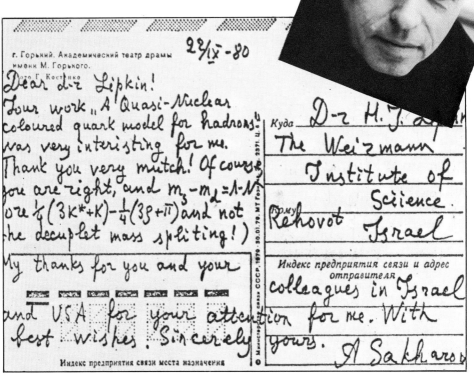

to formulate a theory which would cover *all* the forces of nature at once. At
first his unified field theory needed to combine gravitation and electromagnetism under the same set of equations. By the 1930s there was the
nuclear force to include. In the 1950s, the physicists knew there were two
types of nuclear force, very different in character and strength. A unified
theory must cope with four forces.

For all his efforts, Einstein had no success. Having little truck with
quantum mechanics, he attempted to model the other forces along the
lines of General Relativity. They wouldn't go. In recent years, physicists
actually have had some success in combining the theories of the two
nuclear forces and electromagnetism. They have succeeded where Einstein failed because they have taken the road of quantum mechanics, not
relativity. Einstein's tremendous instinct for physics had sadly gone

astray, and led him up a blind alley for the last forty years of his life. When he died, he also hadn't concluded the decades-long debate with Bohr about chance and causality. He hadn't prevailed, though he was still immovable, certain that he was right. No one else was. But nothing would persuade Einstein that God played at dice.

It was a fitting departure for one of the two greatest minds that natural science has ever known. There had not been a scientist of that stature since Newton's death in 1727. Perhaps to lesser and frailer mortals it brings Einstein nearer to common earth to know that in those last years he once lost his temper. Not about the profoundest problems of physics and philosophy; not about the possibilities of mass annihilation; but about something much closer to a personal quarrel.

He was very angry, abusively angry, when Max Born, one of his oldest and most cherished colleagues, said that he intended to return to Germany for his years of retirement. Einstein couldn't understand or tolerate this. To go and live among those murderers who had slaughtered millions of 'our people'!

For the only time traceable in all Einstein's correspondence, his magnanimity, kindness, even his courtesy deserted him. He had once said that he had no ties at all, not to a nationality, a state, an institution, even a group of friends or family. He was a solitary and all he belonged to was the human race. In old age there was an exception, but one which was discernible much earlier. It is necessary to repeat he wasn't a believing Jew. He had no God except perhaps Spinoza's impersonal God of the cosmos: but in some sense deeper than reason he had come to belong to his people, that is the Jewish people.

Born was upset by the tone of those letters, since he revered Einstein above all men. Einstein would not relent. Nothing in this life, or in the space-time of the universe, would make him forget or forgive the 'final solution'.

It was in his old humane spirit that he issued his warning about world peril, and went on working at his equations the day before he died. (He had an aneurysm, had known for years that death was imminent and thought nothing of it – what was mortality in this universe?)

Others, not so far above the battle as Einstein, accepted more passionately that he was right about the H-bomb. Science had made it possible for the human race to commit suicide. How wide this feeling of fatality spread, no one really knew. But it was there.

9
The younger masters

A spray of atomic debris caused by the chance collision of a cosmic ray into the piston mechanism of a bubble chamber. Cosmic rays are high-speed particles (mostly protons) which bombard the earth from outer space

Meanwhile, particle physics – to a new generation of practitioners still the central subject in physics – was negating the prophecies of its decline. The war had transformed the scale of nuclear experiments. When Cockcroft built his first accelerator, in 1932, it could fit into a small laboratory. Ten years later, the tracks needed to accelerate particles could barely be fitted into an Olympic stadium. That was only the beginning. The cost of experimental research in particle physics rose beyond the financial powers of any European university. The Cavendish gave up the nuclear research which had won it fame. Only government institutes, such as Dubna in Russia, Harwell in England, could afford the new equipment. Rutherford's apparatus had cost a few hundred pounds, Cockcroft's not much more: now the budgets ran into many millions. Experimental nuclear research, and more than half of all the experimental research in the world, of any kind whatever, could be done only in America.

In pure science, America had become by far the greatest force on earth. Great universities, including Stanford, Berkeley, MIT and Princeton, could combine with government agencies to build major nuclear apparatuses. Young scientists went to America as once they had gone to the three European plinths of physics, Cambridge, Göttingen, Copenhagen.

That change, though, was more logistic than vital. Scientists go where they can do their work, and don't repine much about the locality. It is possible that there was a slight loss in the intimate exchange of ideas, though as long as Niels Bohr lived theoreticians still spent longish spells in the cosiness of Copenhagen, and the tradition lasted when his son Aage took over. Otherwise physicists became extravagantly mobile, and their old-fashioned seniors grumbled that they were usually in the air – literally rather than figuratively. No one minded. The subject had its own dynamics, and the young were indifferent to the old customs. They were taking over, and science has always been ruthless with the old.

The Van de Graaff voltage generator used to accelerate protons at Britain's Atomic Energy Research Establishment at Harwell, Berkshire, in 1948

The old, the great men of the 1920s and 1930s, were in fact passing from the scene. Rutherford had died – of a curious medical accident – at sixty-six, in 1937. Einstein survived until 1956, Bohr till 1962, both dying in their late seventies. Like many of their near contemporaries, they didn't cease from trying to promote international agreements about the nuclear bomb – not to much avail, except for scientific debates in organizations like Pugwash. Fermi died of cancer in his fifties, a major loss, his splendid mind unimpaired and now taking a world view. He died a modern scientist's version of a stoical Roman death, taking notes about his disease until very near the end. Oppenheimer also died relatively young – at sixty-two – and also of cancer. Pauli, Schrödinger, Broglie, didn't live into old age. Heinsenberg, who had become head of what once had been called the Kaiser Wilhelm Institute, reached his seventies, as did the Cavendish stars, Cockcroft and Blackett.

Extreme longevity, though, was not an occupational feature of major scientists, as it has often been of visual artists and musicians. Of the heroic era of the 1930s the most eminent practitioners now living (1980) are

Kapitsa in his middle eighties, and Dirac relatively juvenile at seventy-eight. There are, of course, plenty of men who were quite young but influential in the making of the first fission bombs, and still actively at work.

The roll-call of mortality, however, hasn't affected the march of physics. It would be astonishing if it had. Some great men seem irreplaceable. There has been only one Einstein, perhaps only one Bohr. They defy the statistical laws. But in general, the amount of scientific talent in the world must be about the same in any period, and the same applies to anything short of the most abnormal genius. As scientific education spreads to larger numbers of the world's population, as now in China, the number of available talents will increase. The only question is whether the intellectual situation (and other situations too) will give those talents the fullest possible opportunity to flourish. It may be that the circumstances of the 1920s and 1930s were abnormally propitious. Physicists today may not

The building housing the USSR's giant Synchrofasotron, which is capable of producing 10 GeV (milliard electronvolts)

have the same extraordinary opportunity, and it may not have happened before in the history of science. That has been argued by observers of detachment and historical sense.

The argument is well meant; there may be a little in it, but not much. No one would think of doubting that contemporary theoreticians such as Richard Feynman, Murray Gell-Mann, Abdus Salam, Yuval Ne-eman, Freeman Dyson, would have done spectacular work if born just before 1900 and in their prime in the mid 1920s. All that is certain. It is also possible, or even probable, that they might have found it slightly easier to arrive at major conceptions, and formulations, overnight. That is open to reflection. Having said that, one has said about all that is valid on the good or bad luck of being born in 1940 rather than 1900.

The test is, what is felt inside the situation by the contemporary theorists themselves. They show the same creative satisfaction as their forerunners half a century ago. They are as confident. The great problems are showing themselves more difficult than was once thought – all the better. As Rutherford in one letter encouraged Bohr, no one can expect to clear up the whole of physics in a week, and one ought to feel grateful that the enterprise looks like going on for ever.

That has been the view of the toughest-minded physicists of the century. They have enjoyed recalling that Lord Kelvin, the great nineteenth-century classical physicist, announced around 1904 that physics had now come to an end – presumably with himself. Whereas Rabi, asked recently what branch of science he would now devote himself to, if starting today as a young man (the answer expected was probably molecular biology), said with his customary robustness, 'Nuclear physics, of course.'

The present leaders would cheerfully say the same. The theoreticians might add that their recent work hasn't yet been widely assimilated, even among fellow professionals. There has been a longer time-lag than in the assimilation of quantum mechanics. That doesn't matter. Their juniors will make the exposition clearer. All scientific exposition comes to look straightforward within a generation. Richard Feynman is a major scientific figure and that is already recognized.

Feynman has performed one of the great intellectual syntheses, which lives under the general title of quantum electrodynamics. With scientists' addiction to hilarity, it is usually called QED. It is perhaps not an accident that Einstein's paper on the Special Theory of Relativity was originally called 'On the Electrodynamics of Moving Bodies'. Feynman's

Contemporary theoreticians.
Top: Richard Feynman and Murray Gell-Mann.
Above: Yuval Ne'eman and Freeman Dyson

is a generalization on the same scale but looking at the subject from a different point of view.

Einstein had used Maxwell's laws of electromagnetism to investigate the properties of a moving body. He found the well-known bizarre effects of relativity: a moving body becomes shortened; its mass increases; its clocks run slower. Feynman was interested in the details of electromagnetic force itself. In QED, the electric repulsion is not caused by 'action at a distance', or by a 'field' distorting space and time – the path that Einstein was trying to follow in his later years. Electrical and magnetic forces are the result of charged particles exchanging entities called photons. These are in fact none other than the units of radiation, the quanta, that Planck and Einstein had discovered at the turn of the century. Here, however, they are not acting as particles of radiation. They are exchanged so quickly that scientists cannot ever detect them passing from one body to another – Heisenberg's Uncertainty Principle ensures that. But they do produce a force.

Feynman extended this concept until the theory could explain all the remaining puzzles in electricity and magnetism. QED, for example, predicts with amazing accuracy the strength of the electron's magnetic field, a quantity that simpler theories had invariably got wrong. The theory needed much heavier mathematical machinery than anything in the Special Theory of Relativity, some contributed by one of Feynman's collaborators, Freeman Dyson. Dyson is English-born, a man of formidable mathematical powers combined with a whirling imagination. Englishmen might like to say that he is a credit to English education: but he would have been a credit to any education anywhere, that kind of gift being too irrepressible to subdue.

The full importance of quantum electrodynamics has not yet been seen in perspective. The statements are accepted, but at present they look bizarre. Feynman himself looks a little bizarre by comparison with his immediate seniors. Most of them, not all, gave an external appearance of gravitas. Kapitsa, with cheek and psychological subtlety, penetrated Rutherford's façade, but no one else dared to. Bohr was not only a paterfamilias at home but a father figure to anyone around him. Nearly all the others were reasonably stately personages. Of course, some of them had their private troubles and frailties, sexual, even financial, but those didn't obtrude as with a similar assembly of artists. The percentage of stable marriages among scientists has been abnormally high.

Feynman has his own style, and a very different one from Rutherford's or Bohr's. To an extent, it is a style shared by some of his contemporaries. But essentially it is Feynman's own. He would grin at himself if guilty of stately behaviour. He is a showman, and enjoys it. Since he enjoys it, he is not inclined to suppress it. He is a dashing performer. There have been a number of fine and eloquent expositors of science. W. L. Bragg was a splendid lecturer. Feynman is also a splendid lecturer, but in a distinctly different tone, rather as though Groucho Marx was suddenly standing in for a great scientist.

Here we ought to remember that sober-minded observers, such as the philosopher Samuel Alexander, knowing both Rutherford and Einstein when young though already world-famous, decided that Rutherford behaved like a rowdy boy and Einstein like a merry boy. The latter statement is the more interesting, in view of the moral weight that Einstein carried in later life. It may have accrued to him as life darkened him, though even in old age he could burst into bouts of jollity. It will be interesting for young men to meet Feynman in his later years.

All those capable of judging say that the theory of quantum elec-trodynamics is beautiful – a favourite term of theoreticians' praise. In the same spirit, the present theory of sub-atomic particles strikes those inside the situation as beautiful. Outsiders, with appropriate humility, might suggest that it is a fairly rococo kind of beauty.

The memory returns to Heisenberg, in the early 1920s, going for a solitary stroll through the grounds of Bohr's institute, and brooding over the question – can nature be all that absurd? Thirty or forty years later, Heisenberg's successors could have been thinking that nature might not be all that absurd but was singularly lacking in economy. The great new particle accelerators in the United States – giant descendants of Cock-croft's accelerator – propelled sub-atomic particles to higher and higher energies. (Although none can travel as fast as light, the closer they get to that limiting speed, the more energy they have.) These high energy bullets were creating many new, different species of sub-atomic particles when they hit any kind of target. The comparative simplicity of a universe consisting of only three types of particles, protons, electrons, neutrons, had disappeared. These new-found particles existed only for a fraction of a second, but their existence was incontrovertible. All were heavier than the electron, most heavier even than the proton, and they came with different masses and with different charges. Nearly all physicists believed – and still

Section of the CERN accelerator used in the search for charmed particles. Proton beams
are caused to collide, producing quarks and other sub-atomic phenomena

believe – as a matter of intuition or faith, that there must, in the very long
run, be elegance and harmony in nature. A few heretics, like the
immensely talented Edward Bullard, have always been convinced that
this is a man-made or anthropomorphic delusion. For nearly everyone
else, though, there had in the end, so they felt, to be elegance and
harmony. In this new medley of particles, where had the elegance and
harmony gone?

Some of the most powerful of the new generation of theoreticians
weren't defeated, notably Murray Gell-Mann and his colleague Yuval
Ne-eman. Yes, there *was* an underlying harmony and an underlying
beauty, but it needed new concepts and new mathematics to read it. The
new mathematics which Gell-Mann introduced was more unfamiliar
than the matrix algebra which had founded quantum mechanics, and was
more difficult for physicists to domesticate. If experience is any guide, that
domestication will duly happen.

The new mathematical tool that Gell-Mann introduced to physics was
called 'group theory'. As had happened with quantum mechanics and

View of the CERN facilities on the Swiss-French border
near Geneva. The white outline indicates the position of
the underground 400 GeV Super Proton Synchroton

matrix theory, the mathematical structure had been around for a century. It had been formulated by a young French mathematician, Evariste Galois, who wrote out his ideas the night before he was due to take part in a duel. Galois was killed. But his ideas lived on, eventually to form the basis of our current understanding of the particles from which the universe is built up.

Gell-Mann noticed certain patterns amongst the newly discovered particles, when their properties were displayed on a graph. They seemed to fall into certain families, or groups. Galois's group theory applied

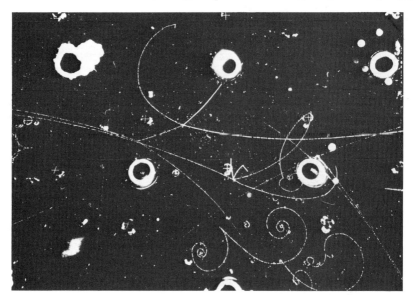

Bubble chamber activity indicating the presence of anti-particles. These have the exact opposite properties of ordinary particles

exactly to this kind of mathematical set-up. Although other physicists were sceptical about Gell-Mann's patterns, he pointed out that the theory indicated a hole, a place in the pattern which should be occupied by a particle with certain properties. In 1964, experimenters at Brookhaven National Laboratory discovered this particle. Gell-Mann was right. The fundamental particles do form families.

Group theory was a stronger tool than this, though. It laid down rules governing the relationships in the family groups: how you would need to alter one particle to turn it into another of the same family or pattern. Gell-Mann found that this mathematical device, which evidently worked

The pressurized water reactor at Fessenheim in France runs on enriched uranium and is cooled by the waters of the Rhine

Professor Abdus Salam

so well, corresponded to a simple physical interpretation. The 'fundamental particles' produced in the particle accelerators are composite. They are made up of smaller entities, which Gell-Mann called 'quarks' – apparently before he detected that peculiarly unsuitable word in *Finnegan's Wake*. Gell-Mann is deeply cultivated, an enthusiastic linguist, one of the cleverest men of the century as well as one of the deepest conceptual thinkers; but like nature itself he hasn't much taste for classical austerity.

Quarks are very curious entities, if entity is the right word. They come either in twos or threes, the latter cutting across the grain of nearly all natural phenomena. Three quarks make up one proton. Quarks are not individually detectable by experimental means: they exist, but in the formal world of the new equations. They exhibit various phases of behaviour in those equations, to which theoreticians have attached terms of discrimination, such as colour, flavour, charm. These terms mean nothing except as labels in the equations themselves.

There has been nothing quite like this array of concepts in theoretical physics, or in any other branch of science before. It presents some absorbing problems in epistemology. If Einstein and Bohr were still alive, that great debate of theirs would take on another lease of existence. Theory has reached a climactic point – this is the present climax, and not the final one, of a series of revolutions which began in 1900 with Planck and his quantum of radiation, climbed up to the heights of Einstein and Bohr, consolidated itself with Dirac and Heisenberg, as always in science drawing in many minds along the way, and is now expressed by Gell-Mann, Ne-eman, Salam, and a dozen others.

Those who have contributed to this intellectual edifice – it is not a rhetorical flourish to say with a cool mind that it is the major intellectual achievement of our century, and will be so regarded by our successors – have come from nearly all countries, different forms of society, different ethnic stocks. The names in this account tell their own story. There have been Americans, Russians, Germans, French, Italians, British, Japanese. A statistically disproportionate number are of Jewish origin.

There is someone who ranks with the most eminent who should be mentioned. This is Abdus Salam, who has over the past twenty-five years been a leader in the theoretical developments just discussed. Salam was born in a peasant home in a Pakistani village. He managed to get a place in the government college at Lahore. Conceptual and mathematical ability is easy to detect at a very early age, and in Salam's case some enlightened administrator apparently did so. After Lahore, he was despatched to Cambridge, studied with Dirac, and since then has had a creative career of continuous brilliance.

He is a citizen of the world and has devoted much of his influence and energy to help educate young scientists who come from provenances as underprivileged as his own. To this end he established the International Centre for Theoretical Physics, an institute which has its home in Trieste, thanks to the goodwill of the Italian authorities, and Salam has vigorously commuted between the Adriatic and his home and professorship at King's College in London. The Centre has had many successes in developing the progress of scientists of all races. Few men have done more good than Salam for the talented poor.

It happens that Salam is a devout Moslem, believing passionately in the highest axiom of Islam, the essential brotherhood of man. It is good for us to be reminded that men like Salam can translate this axiom into action.

Incidentally, Salam is probably the only committed religious believer, in the doctrinal sense, among all the great theoreticians. Many have had deep religious feelings, as Einstein had, but couldn't accept any creed or belief. Most were reverent in the face of nature, had their own personal morality, sometimes a piety towards the religion in which they had been brought up, but in which they ceased to find meaning. But Salam is, in the full sense, a religious man.

10
A different harvest

Experimental radar installation used by the defence establishment to monitor the movement of air traffic over Britain

The story of particle physics continues unabated at the present day. In spite of the 1945 gloom, the 'beautiful subject' has gone on with surprises and consequences. But there have been other developments, outside the mainstream of the nuclear explorations, which deserve treatment on their own, not only for their intrinsic interest, but because they may prove to affect human lives more than any of the military applications of nuclear energy. Although most of these had roots dating back before the war, it is only in the last three decades that they have come to affect our everyday lives. All that can be done here is to make a number of perfunctory notes.

In the 1939–45 war a high proportion of physicists (in Britain something like 80 per cent) detached themselves from their own researches and were diverted to radar. Many of them adapted themselves with ease. If you could do one kind of physics, you could do another. They learned about the possibilities of electronics. The same transmutation happened in America, and to an extent in Germany – though, for reasons which are still not completely understood, the German use of scientists was nothing like so thorough as their use in the English-speaking world. In Britain, this concentration on electronics was good war-making. For years, it seemed the only salvation.

When the war ended, it was obvious to many good scientists that the same process could be used the other way round. If you had learned about electronics, you could take it straight into pure science. That was how the British launched into a new domain, which we now know of as radio astronomy. In wartime established scientists like Martin Ryle and Bernard Lovell, and others slightly junior – J. S. Hey, Antony Hewish, and a good many others – had studied the detection of radio waves. (They had all made important contributions to the development of radar weapons.) It was natural to turn that kind of technique and thinking to radio waves in the cosmos. A flood of discoveries followed, right up to the present day. The techniques of radio astronomy were picked up all over the world.

The meaning of some of the discoveries was argued about with considerable passion, as was anything to do with cosmology. Those controversies will go rumbling on. But it became apparent that, just as the microscopic universe of sub-atomic particles was proving weirder than anyone had imagined, so was the macrocosmic universe of stars and galaxies.

Some of the thoughts about the microcosm brought illumination to the macrocosm, and the reverse. The annihilation of matter, the identity of matter and energy, the existence of anti-matter, had all had a conceptual pre-figuring in the equations of Einstein, Dirac and other theoreticians of the immediate past. Now, in some interpretations of the astronomical data, one can see them happen. The only way to explain the phenomenal energy of the quasars is by matter turning into energy. And Einstein had predicted that in compact objects gravity could become so strong that nothing could escape: astronomers now have evidence that such black holes really do exist.

These findings are going to give a sense of wonder for long enough. To some of the speculations, there may not be an answer. Pessimistic scientists have been known to say that not only is the universe weirder than we can now understand, it may be weirder than we shall ever understand. That meant that there are kinds of comprehension which we can't transcend. That, however, remains very much a minority view.

In our immediate period, say 1950–80, physicists have also made sensational inroads into biological problems. Crystallography had always been off the mainstream of modern physics. It deals, not with the structure of nuclei and atoms, but with the geography of atoms – the position of atoms in solid matter, and recently, and far more difficult, in liquid matter also. Crystallography is not only an elegant study, but one with multifarious uses. However, the nuclear scientists didn't consider it was touching the core of physics. Rutherford didn't permit it to enter the Cavendish. It might be slightly more respectable than spectroscopy, Kapitsa remarked, but both were like putting things into boxes, or perhaps a form of stamp-collecting.

Nevertheless, W. L. Bragg (later Sir Laurence), whom everyone agreed was a scientist of the highest class, had devoted his scientific life to the subject. So did another man of great gifts, J. D. Bernal. Although chemists and geologists had been looking at the exterior forms of crystals for centuries, Bragg and Bernal could bring a twentieth-century technique to bear on the fundamental atomic structure of crystals. The key was X-rays. X-rays are radiation, like light, but with a much shorter wavelength. X-ray wavelengths – at around a ten-thousand-millionth of a metre – are very similar to the spacing between atoms in a crystal. When X-rays shine on a crystal they penetrate it. But some are reflected back from the different layers and rows of atoms, and the reflected pattern gives clues to the atomic structures within the crystal. The patterns are not easy to read. It requires an experienced judgement, or complex computer programmes that have only been available in the past few years. But in principle, all the information is there, cryptically, in the pattern of reflected X-rays.

As early as the 1930s, Bragg and Bernal and their colleagues were considering ways of applying X-ray crystallographic techniques to some of the crucial problems of biology, among them the structure of the genetic material, the molecules within the living cell that determine its structure, and pass on information so that its descendants are similarly constructed. At that time, the full range of crystallographic techniques was not ready for the purpose, but the intellectual foresight was.

By the 1950s, the techniques were ripe. Experimental results on DNA (deoxyribonucleic acid) – now known to be the genetic material – were accumulating. The scientists who interpreted it, who showed that the DNA molecule is twisted around itself, were Francis Crick and James Watson. Watson's *The Double Helix* is a brilliant book and has permanent value as showing that scientists are human, or, if you like, only too human. It was generously welcomed, and by Bragg himself with supreme magnanimity. Bragg, like Einstein and Bohr, was one of the saints of science. In cool retrospect, though, the book would be more acceptable if it showed more recognition of the cumulative nature of science. To repeat what has been said already, science is an edifice. To put in a brick, a scientist has to climb on the shoulders of other men, often greater men. Individuals, except for the odd anomaly who occurs once in a hundred years, don't count all that much. Both Bragg and Bernal, who knew a lot about the history of science, would have accepted that without reserve. But if one is writing a history of a specific discovery at a specific time as with DNA, it would be a distortion to leave those two out.

That said, it was a very great discovery, and will have, when the lesson

Model of the double helix structure of the DNA molecule

Francis Crick (above), James Watson (top left), and Maurice Wilkins, joint winners of the 1962 Nobel prize for medicine and physiology

has sunk in, perhaps in a generation or two, profound – and to many disturbing – human consequences. Human vanity will not be quite the same, nor some of the more ill-founded human hopes.

Francis Crick was a physicist by training, and had spent the war as a somewhat discontented member of one of the radar teams. Once released, he beat around for something worth doing. As it were not by second nature but by first, he had a deep sense of what was important and what might be soluble. Those two things are, of course, not the same, but a great scientist nosing his way into unexplored territory needs them both. Rutherford had that combination to the highest degree. A number of marvellously accomplished scientists haven't had it at all. As an example, there is the sad life of Einstein's closest friend and the only one he turned to for criticism, Paul Ehrenfest. Ehrenfest was a brilliant theoretician, but all his contributions were to the more abstruse branches of physics. Crick does have the necessary combination, and it was the greatest of his gifts, although for his particular gamble he needed also comprehensive intelligence and fighting spirit.

He didn't know much crystallography, and never became a supreme practitioner as Bragg and Bernal were. He learned enough for his purposes. He didn't know much biology but decided that he didn't need to know much. Unravelling the secrets of DNA was a problem where it did more harm than good to be cluttered up with preconceptions. What he did know was that once the material structure of DNA was established by X-ray crystallography, then one ought to be able to make sense out of it.

Then Watson came along, who had another of the valuable gifts, that is an eye for a winner. Each had part of the story. The rest one can learn, or infer, from Watson's book. There are some obvious points. Rosalind Franklin didn't get a fair deal – the Nobel prize was shared between Crick, Watson and Maurice Wilkins, who had performed the vital X-ray experiments. Bernal used to say that the Nobel prize should have been split two ways, Crick and Franklin as one pair, Watson and Wilkins as the other. This would have had the advantage that Crick, good with women, would have been protective of Rosalind Franklin, who wasn't easy to look after.

Another point is very clear – if Crick and Watson hadn't got there, and published, it wouldn't have been long, possibly only weeks, certainly not more than months, before others did. Linus Pauling in America was very nearly there, and one fresh look might have clinched it. It was a case even more striking than the Special Theory of Relativity. Several minds were converging on the same solution – and understanding DNA didn't require as much conceptual apparatus as the Special Theory.

Yet there was no injustice about anything that accrued to Crick. His later work on the genetic code – the way that information is actually stored in the DNA molecule – was a feat of extreme intellectual skill and major significance. Here again there was a convergence. In the United States, Joshua Lederberg was reaching the same conclusions independently. Now the instructions for life are understood, genetic engineering enables man to make new kinds of living cells, to produce huge quantities of useful drugs. 'Biotechnology' is becoming a major new industry. Philosophically, the ability to alter the basis of life at will may have even more effect. The meaning of this work hasn't sunk into popular consciousness, even among intellectual persons, with anything like the rapidity of Darwin's *On the Origin of Species*. In the long run it may do as much or more to alter men's view of themselves.

That, though, will have to wait until the twenty-first century. What will not have to wait until the twenty-first century, but is hitting the industrialized world here and now, is the recent domestication of electronics. For many years, it had been realized that there were great numbers of operations which men had to perform, mechanical, laborious, repetitive, which ought to be given over to machines. This was true of mental operations as well as physical. Routine calculations could be done faster and more efficiently by a mechanical process than by a human mind. Bold thinkers speculated that there could be mechanical memories, more comprehensive than human ones.

There was nothing wrong with the idea. The crippling difficulty was that no one could devise a machine for any such purpose which would work anything like fast enough. Charles Babbage, a fine Victorian mathematician with an inventive flair, actually thought out and constructed a machine we now call a computer. In principle he was completely right. But his machine worked by mechanical energy and that was too slow by an order of magnitude.

Brilliant ideas have often had to wait for new techniques, but the reverse is also true: new techniques have often led to brilliant ideas. It was not until electrons, and electronic currents, began to be understood that there was any chance of a workable Babbage machine. It took a long time, technological ingenuity, concentration upon gadgets and, finally, the

pressure of war. As a young man, Rutherford transmitted radio waves over a mile in Cambridge. But he immediately gave that up as a plaything, too remote from the heart of physics. It took an inventor like Marconi to persist, and make radio a commercial proposition. Improved electronic valves were an industrial development. Electronic circuits were to physicists a complicated study, but not profound – the kind of topic they shied from. To see their fundamental significance needed not only inventive ingenuity, but mathematical insight.

At last that happened, and very fast, during the 1939–45 war. Mainly for the purposes of cryptographic decoding, a secret incomparably better kept than the nuclear bomb, computers, primitive by today's standards but just as functional, were being built. Some of the acutest minds in the Western world were at work: not world-comprehensive minds like Einstein's, but minds with a peculiarly rare specific gift. There were a number. In America there was the one-time infant prodigy, John von Neumann, born in Budapest; in England the hero was Alan Turing, whose intellect did more practical service to the country than could be credited to most household names of that war. Turing was the nearest English approach to the great von Neumann.

From that time on it was beginning to be realized that computers were going to take over a good many aspects of workaday existence. In fact, there has been too much mystification about them. They can perform many tasks which human intelligence can't: but they are of course useless without human intelligence. After all, they can always be unplugged. In memory storage, they can be given masses of facts which no human memory can retain, reproduce them when given the necessary instructions, do with precision what they are told. And yet, even there, they can't have the fluidity and range of a decent human memory, for which, in many commonplace tasks as well as all creative ones, there is no substitute.

It is silly to be frightened by computers. Nevertheless, the social impact is bound to be cumulative. That is already evident all over the industrialized world, in North America, Europe, the USSR, Japan, and increasingly in parts of the Far East. Incidentally, Japan is worth particular notice. The Japanese scientists, technologists, technocrats, have shown skills and originality in all this electronic apotheosis which quite out-class the West's. That ought to surprise no one who has given the most perfunctory attention to Japanese visual art or literature or pure science.

The culmination of Marconi's work – the largest steerable radio telescope in the world. *Inset:* Marconi adjusting the telephone and telegraph receiver of the Vatican short-wave station in 1931

For hundreds of years the culture has been wildly original, something oddly different from any other among the sons of men. It was an instance of Western blindness not to discover that simple fact.

All over the industrialized world, then, computers – using the term as shorthand for all forms of automatic guidance and control – are spreading. Something else is spreading. That is the realization that nearly all the goods that this industrialized world is now producing – which means an enormous proportion of all the goods produced on our planet – could, with such technological knowledge and a little organization, be made by not more than 40 per cent of the present labour force. Even with the present organization, industrial production, which includes modern agriculture, requires nothing like the number of workers who are now employed. If we considered nothing but functional needs, then the advanced societies of the world are already masking a high level of unemployment.

That will increase, and dramatically increase, on account of the newest, quietest, and most irreversible of technological revolutions. This is the extension of electronic control right down to the domestic scale. Computers were constructed as soon as complex electronic circuits were feasible. It has been discovered that what are in effect miniature computers can be constructed, without electronic valves at all, and without any of the labyrinthine paraphernalia. There was an element of chance in this discovery, but it came through researches into the curious properties of what are known as semi-conductors, in which electrons can travel, but not with the freedom with which they travel in metals. The element silicon is a semi-conductor. Slivers of silicon can be made into perfectly effective mini-computers which can be carried like a map in a pocket diary. And recently, and even more bizarre, it has been found that a substance previously unknown to fame, gallium arsenide, is even better fitted for the job. Silicon chips will soon be replaced by this hitherto obscure compound which has the peculiar ability to emit light like a miniature laser. There must be other comparable semi-conductors. Rapid searches are presumably being made through textbooks of inorganic chemistry.

None of this sounds specially catastrophic, by the side of nuclear explosions, or even the first blundering waves of the Industrial Revolution. Yet, as was hinted in the first section of this account, it casts a shadow before it. It is likely to affect human life – and immediately in our industrialized world – more than any of those events. For a simple reason. At present, as has just been mentioned, the industrialized world can

A wafer of unseparated silicon chips next to a watch movement.
Microcomputers are capable of increasingly complex tasks, such as control
of small switching exchanges, traffic flow, and washing machines. With
increasing miniaturization, molecular-sized circuits are now a possibility

Man Lying on a Wall, by L. S. Lowry
Opposite: An IBM computer machine in Mainz making parts for new
computer machines

produce all it now produces with a fraction of the work-force. With these
mini-processors now to hand, that fraction could, and in some societies
certainly will, almost at once be reduced, not just slightly, but by – what?
Half? Three-quarters? If production alone is the measure, more than that.

This lack of need for workers applies to productive industry, not
everywhere. Service industries cannot be worked to the same extent by
these subtle devices. The trouble is, as we already know all over the
industrialized world, there can be destructive unemployment in productive industry, and simultaneously a corresponding demand in service
industry. People insist on their old jobs in factories where they are now
obsolete: at the same time they are not prepared to be postmen. If service
industries paid more than factories the problem would still not disappear.

That dilemma is going to be sharpened by this most recent gift of
applied physics. The curse of labour, laid on man after the Fall, is for
many ready to be taken away. Like other gifts, this one may be two-edged
or have two faces.

11
The double legacy

Civil Defence workers in New York during a mock nuclear alert staged in
major American cities in 1955

This century, then, has not just been the triumphant age of pure physics. The successes achieved by pure physics will continue. Prediction in science, as Peter Medawar has often told us, is by definition impossible: but it will be a puzzle if those alive in fifty years' time haven't seen this process continuing and cumulative. They will understand more than anyone can now imagine.

But this is also a century that has seen the profound practical results of the physicists' triumphs. There are some which lurk in the minds of reflective persons. One, which has been touched on in the last chapter, is the effect of micro-processors on industrial living everywhere. This still, in 1980, hasn't clearly entered the public consciousness. In this year, we haven't yet recognized what is going to hit us. We shall. For the moment, or for this account, we had better leave it there.

The other profound result is that reflective persons – and persons not usually reflective – have been living with anxiety. Here there has been a recognition, dark, looming, that something really might hit us – the something being, of course, the supreme technical accomplishment, the fusion (hydrogen) bomb. The questions in many minds have been 'if' and 'when'. Is there going to be a nuclear war? When will it happen?

That dread has been hanging over us for thirty-five years, which is a long time in modern history. It wouldn't have been candid not to mention it in the first words of this book. It will continue to darken thoughts of the future for a long time yet. Some have doubted whether there is going to be a future.

And yet, it is possible to suggest that this may not be realistic. Of all the dangers in front of us, it may very well be that nuclear war is the least likely. It doesn't need saying that our world is precarious. It will remain so. But there is a subdued irony. It might have been more precarious if the hydrogen bomb had never been made. For the past thirty-five years, the two super-powers, and all others involved, have been divided by suspicion

Inside the control point of an H-bomb range. A technician sits at the computer
console awaiting the countdown signal to push the button that detonates the bomb

almost absolute, and by distrust even stronger than suspicion. They have
exchanged insults and abuse which, by any previous precedent, would
have been near declarations of war, and sometimes nearer than that. Just
remember the diplomatic to-ing and fro-ing which set in motion (as if by
Einstein's 'weird inevitability') the 1914–18 war. The language and the
protests were mild compared with what we now read in each morning's
paper. Austria finally sent an ultimatum to Serbia. That didn't affect real
power relations any more than if America today sent an ultimatum to
Cuba. At that time, it immediately led to a cataclysmic war. We have
come through more articulate conflicts than that in the present in at least
superficial peace. That is due to the mutual threat of nuclear bombs.

Far-sighted military commentators realized, soon after such bombs
were made, that they had one curious property. Granted that both sides
had enough to inflict 'unacceptable' damage, it was going to be impossible
for sane governments or commanders to use them.

This is a peculiarity possessed by no other weapon of war ever made. What is 'unacceptable' damage? Here an Englishman can comment with a certain detachment. It happens that, owing to the small size of Britain, the density of population, and the extreme articulation of the whole organism, the country would be more easily destroyed in nuclear war than any other sizeable power. During one of the meetings between Harold Macmillan and President Kennedy, the British Prime Minister wished to illustrate this point. He summoned his chief expert on nuclear weapons, William Penney. 'Sir William, would you please tell the President how many hydrogen bombs would be needed to finish our country off?' Penney answered: 'Five, I should think, Prime Minister.' Pause for reflection, and Penney continued: 'Oh, just to be on the safe side, let's say eight.'

Just to be on the safe side: those words will make a neat footnote to history. But what is true for Britain doesn't begin to apply to the United States and the Soviet Union. The United States is a very large expanse. The Soviet Union is much larger. Both sides could, in theory, inflict about the same amount of annihilation. That will remain true. There will be no

Representatives of foreign countries taking part
in the nuclear disarmament campaign march
from Aldermaston to London in April 1960

Direction of blast

2a

Damage at about 4 - 5 miles from ground-burst 10 m.t. bomb (=500n)

British Civil Defence information poster, 1958

help from new gadgets or technological differences. The only prospect of survival would be through the wide distribution of the population over those great areas. In this grisly arithmetic, anyone's guess is about as good as anyone else's. Things go askew in war, and it seems likely that estimates of something like total annihilation on both sides are an exaggeration. To destroy half of all Americans and half of all Soviet people would seem nearer to what nuclear exchanges could do.

Is that unacceptable, to use the egregious military terminology again? Probably: even more so, since that preliminary exchange would almost certainly be succeeded by a particularly atrocious land war with 'conventional' weapons. These calculations have to be made by military commanders and politicians. Unless the world goes even madder than the most pessimistic expect, that particular doomsday doesn't appear within the range of our potential fate.

One side comment. Nuclear war between the super-powers will continue to remain a dread, like a fear of mortal disease, but will also continue to have a low degree of probability. That, unfortunately, is not true of minor nuclear wars, as more countries come to possess the bombs. In addition to the super-powers, Britain, France, and China have demonstrated that they have them. At least two other countries certainly have them also, and very likely three or four more already. These bombs are not too difficult to make, which is a pity. In favourable circumstances, where the constraints of the super-powers did not operate, they might be used.

That is a more realistic worry than the prospect of nuclear war between the super-powers. So is the thought of such bombs getting into the hands of terrorists. These are minor anxieties by the side of the major one which has weighed on so many for so long. But these anxieties exist, and they are a negative legacy of the physicists' triumph.

Applied science, however, is two-faced. There is likely to be another, and a very great, positive legacy from that same scientific triumph. There is a chance, and a good one, that humankind will within the lifetime of today's children be certain of their supplies of energy forever. Forever is a long time: perhaps it would be better to say until the seas run dry or until the human species has had a transmutation. Which, since there is a rough rule that species tend to change in a million years, gives a nice comfortable stretch ahead.

This chance, of the answer to the problem of energy, comes from the identical mechanism which produces the hydrogen bomb. The process is

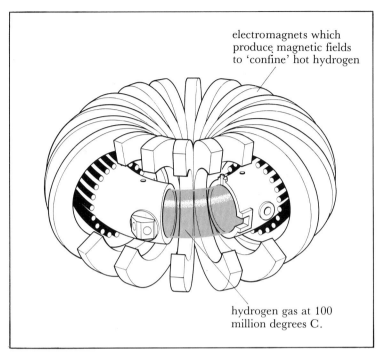

electromagnets which produce magnetic fields to 'confine' hot hydrogen

hydrogen gas at 100 million degrees C.

A tokamak for nuclear fusion (cutaway)

the fusion of hydrogen nuclei to make up helium nuclei. It is the way in which the sun makes its own continuous output of energy. In the hydrogen bomb, the fusion produces – by terrestrial standards – a very large but indiscriminate and uncontrolled outburst of energy. If this can be controlled, and domesticated for workaday uses, then the major practical problem of how to keep the human race fed and warmed and physically equipped, no longer exists. Fossil fuels – oil, coal – will be exhausted in an uncomfortably short time: we have wasted them with the utmost carelessness. With fusion energy as a source, the only need is hydrogen. Although hydrogen gas is not found free on our planet, the oceans are full of it, for water is made of two atoms of hydrogen to one of oxygen. There will be no side-products and nothing to disturb the apprehensive.

That is the prospect. It is the most glowing material prospect which has ever been dangled before us. It is as well to cross our fingers, touch wood, knock on wood, or do whatever our various superstitions tell us to do with wood. Controlling fusion energy is the most difficult job that applied physics or physical-engineering has yet been given. The technological

Windscale, Britain's prototype advanced gas cooled reactor near Whitehaven in Cumbria. By the early 1990s about 30 per cent of the nation's energy needs will be supplied by nuclear power

problems are vast, such as raising the hydrogen gas to a temperature of a hundred million degrees, the temperature needed to start the fusion reaction.

There are a good many people working on the project in America, the Soviet Union, and Britain, and the international exchange has been close. These people have been kept going by hope, faith, and reason. Which has been the most useful impulse would be hard to say. The faith is that there hasn't been a technological problem, certainly not one of supreme significance, to which an answer hasn't in due course been found. Various different attempts were started in the three countries shortly after the war. Within a few years the British believed that, in principle, they had done it. They shouted too soon. Men, usually level-headed, temporarily lost their judgement. Judicious Americans said that they were disappointed in the British: this wasn't their traditional behaviour. But perhaps there was some excuse. After all, this was the most tremendous of all scientific prizes.

That was a false start. More recently, the Soviet scientists, who had been following two radically dissimilar lines, discovered one that was promising, maybe more than promising. It has been christened by the acronym 'tokamak'. The Americans, who were following a similar path, took up tokamak with vigour, using, as a pleasant cordiality, the same nickname. There had been signs, still being argued about, of a step forward. The tokamak is a ring-shaped tube, like a hollow doughnut. Magnetic fields keep the super-hot hydrogen at the central axis of the tube, so that it cannot touch the metal walls and burn its way out. Another, completely different, approach to fusion power is to package the hydrogen into small pellets only a few millimetres across, and blast them from all sides with laser power or beams of electrons.

At present, no outsider could say more about the state of fusion power with meaning, and the insiders, if they can, prefer not to. It may be years before they know for sure, and longer before either society gets to work on practical engineering. The cost, to begin with, will be stupendous but the rewards will be stupendous too.

What the physicists have done, speaks for itself. It would be jejune to add anything. Their own intellectual structure waits there to be added to, but is unshakeable. The application which has come out of that structure has left us with some threats and more promises. It is for the general intelligence of us all to make the best of both.

Appendices

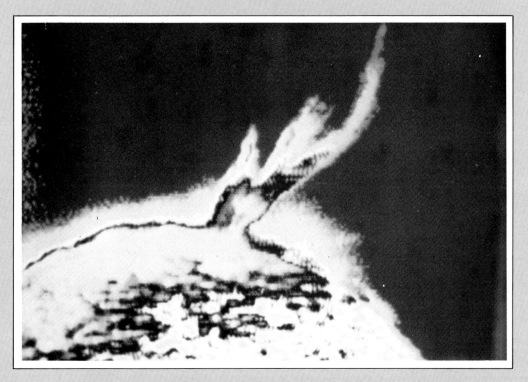

Solar flare. At the sun's core hydrogen nuclei fuse to make helium nuclei.
The energy is liberated as sunshine

1 A new means of destruction

Editorial by C. P. Snow in Discovery, *September 1939*

Some physicists think that, within a few months, science will have produced for military use an explosive a million times more violent than dynamite. It is no secret; laboratories in the United States, Germany, France and England have been working on it feverishly since the Spring. It may not come off. The most competent opinion is divided upon whether the idea is practicable. If it is, science for the first time will at one bound have altered the scope of warfare. The power of most scientific weapons has been consistently exaggerated; but it would be difficult to exaggerate this.

So there are two questions. *Will* it come off? How will the world be affected if it does?

As to the practicability, most of our opinions are worth little. The most eminent physicist with whom I have discussed it thinks it improbable; I have talked to others who think it as good as done. In America, as soon as the possibility came to light, it seemed so urgent that a representative of American physicists telephoned the White House and arranged an interview with the President. That was about three months ago. And it is in America where the thing will in all probability be done, if it is done at all.

The principle is fairly simple, and is discussed by Mr D. W. F. Mayer in more detail on p. 459. Briefly, it is this: a slow neutron knocks a uranium nucleus into two approximately equal pieces, and two or more *faster* neutrons are discharged at the same time. These faster neutrons go on to disintegrate other uranium nuclei, and the process is self-accelerating. It is the old dream of the release of intra-atomic energy, suddenly made actual at a time when most scientists had long discarded it; energy is *gained* by the trigger action of the first neutrons.

The idea of the uranium bomb is to disintegrate in this manner an entire lump of uranium. As I have said, many physicists of sound judgement consider that the technical difficulties have already been removed; but their critics ask – if this scheme were really workable, why have not the great uranium mines (the biggest are in Canada and the Congo) blown themselves up long ago? The percentage of uranium in pitchblende is very high: and there are always enough neutrons about to set such a trigger action going.

Well, in such a scientific controversy, with some of the ablest physicists in the world on each side, it would be presumptuous to intrude. But on the result there may depend a good many lives, and perhaps more than that.

For what will happen, if a new means of destruction, far more effective than any now existing, comes into our hands? I think most of us, certainly those working day and night this summer upon the problem in New York, are pessimistic about the result. We have seen too much of human selfishness and frailty to pretend that men can be trusted with a new weapon of gigantic power. Most scientists are by temperament fairly hopeful and simple-minded about political things: but in the last eight years that hope has been drained away. In our time, at least, life has been impoverished, and not enriched, by the invention of flight. We cannot delude ourselves that this new invention will be better used.

Yet it must be made, if it really is a physical possibility. If it is not made in America this year, it may be next year in Germany. There is no ethical problem; if the invention is not prevented by physical laws, it will certainly be carried out somewhere in the world. It is better, at any rate, that America should have six months' start.

But again, we must not pretend. Such an invention will never be kept secret; the physical principles are too obvious, and within a year every big laboratory on earth would have come to the same result. For a short time, perhaps, the U.S. Government may have this power entrusted to it; but soon after it will be in less civilized hands.

THE EDITOR

II Einstein's letter to President Roosevelt

Albert Einstein
Old Grove Rd.
Nassau Point
Peconic, Long Island

August 2nd, 1939

F. D. Roosevelt,
President of the United States,
White House
Washington, D.C.

Sir:

Some recent work by E. Fermi and L. Szilard, which has been communicated to me in manuscript, leads me to expect that the element uranium may be turned into a new and important source of energy in the immediate future. Certain aspects of the situation which has arisen seem to call for watchfulness and, if necessary, quick action on the part of the Administration. I believe therefore that it is my duty to bring to your attention the following facts and recommendations:

In the course of the last four months it has been made probable – through the work of Joliot in France as well as Fermi and Szilard in America – that it may become possible to set up a nuclear chain reaction in a large mass of uranium, by which vast amounts of power and large quantities of new radium-like elements would be generated. Now it appears almost certain that this could be achieved in the immediate future.

This new phenomenon would also lead to the construction of bombs, and it is conceivable – though much less certain – that extremely powerful bombs of a new type may thus be constructed. A single bomb of this type, carried by boat and exploded in a port, might very well destroy the whole port together with some of the surrounding territory. However, such bombs might very well prove to be too heavy for transportation by air.

The United States has only very poor ores of uranium in moderate quantities. There is some good ore in Canada and the former Czechoslovakia, while the most important source of uranium is Belgian Congo.

In view of this situation you may think it desirable to have some permanent contact maintained between the Administration and the group of physicists working on chain reactions in America. One possible way of achieving this might be for you to entrust with this task a person who has your confidence and who could perhaps serve in an inofficial capacity. His task might comprise the following:

a) to approach Government Departments, keep them informed of the further development, and put forward recommendations for Government action, giving particular attention to the problem of securing a supply of uranium ore for the United States;

b) to speed up the experimental work, which is at present being carried on within the limits of the budgets of University laboratories, by providing funds, if such funds be required, through his contacts with private persons who are willing to make contributions for this cause, and perhaps also by obtaining the co-operation of industrial laboratories which have the necessary equipment.

I understand that Germany has actually stopped the sale of uranium from the Czechoslovakian mines which she has taken over. That she should have taken such early action might perhaps be understood on the ground that the son of the German Under-Secretary of State, von Weizsäcker, is attached to the Kaiser-Wilhelm-Institut in Berlin where some of the American work on uranium is now being repeated.

Yours very truly,

(Albert Einstein)

III The moral un-neutrality of science

Speech by C. P. Snow delivered in 1960 to the American Association for the Advancement of Science

Scientists are the most important occupational group in the world today. At this moment, what they do is of passionate concern to the whole of human society. At this moment, the scientists have little influence on the world effect of what they do. Yet, potentially, they can have great influence. The rest of the world is frightened both of what they do – that is, the intellectual discoveries of science – and of its effect. The rest of the world, transferring its fears, is frightened of the scientists themselves and tends to think of them as radically different from other men.

As an ex-scientist, if I may call myself so, I know that is nonsense. I have even tried to express in fiction some kinds of scientific temperament and scientific experience. I know well enough that scientists are very much like other men. After all, we're all human, even if some of us don't look it. I think I would be prepared to risk a generalization. The scientists I have known – and because of my official life I think I've known as many as anyone in the world – have been in certain respects at least as morally admirable as most other groups of intelligent men.

That is a sweeping statement and I mean it only in a statistical sense. But I think there is just a little in it. The moral qualities I admire in scientists are quite simple ones, but I am very suspicious of attempts to over-subtilize moral qualities. It is nearly always a sign, not of true sophistication, but of a specific kind of triviality. So I admire in scientists very simple virtues – like courage, truth-telling, kindness – in which, judged by the low standards which the rest of us manage to achieve, the scientists are not deficient. I think on the whole the scientists make slightly better husbands and fathers than most of us, and I admire them for it. I don't know the figures, and I should be curious to have them sorted out, but I am prepared to bet that the proportion of divorces among scientists is slightly but significantly less than that among other groups of similar education and income. I do not apologize for considering that a good thing.

A close friend of mine is a very distinguished scientist. He is also one of the few scientists I know who have lived what we used to call a Bohemian life. When we were both younger, he thought he would undertake historical research to see how many great scientists had been as miscellaneously fond of women as he was. I think he would have felt mildly supported if he could have found a precedent. I remember his reporting to me that his researches hadn't had any luck. The really great scientists were depressingly 'normal'. The only gleam of comfort was in the life of Jerome Cardan; and Cardan just wasn't anything like enough to outweigh all the others.

So scientists are not much different from other men. They are certainly no worse than other men. But they do differ from other men in one thing. That is the point I started from. Whether they like it or not, what they do is of critical importance for the human race. Intellectually, it has transformed the climate of our time. Socially, it will decide whether we live or die, and how we live or die. It holds decisive powers for good and evil. *That* is the situation in which the scientists find themselves. They may not have asked for it, or may only have asked for it in part, but they cannot escape it. They think, many of the more sensitive of them, that they don't deserve to have this weight of responsibility heaved upon them. All they want to do is get on with their work. I sympathize. But the scientists can't escape the responsibility – any more than they, or the rest of us, can escape the gravity of the moment in which we stand.

There is, of course, one way to contract out. It has been a favourite way for intellectual persons caught in the midst of water too rough for them.

It consists of the invention of categories – or, if you like, of the division of moral labour. That is, the scientists who want to contract out say, *we* produce the tools. *We* stop there. It is for *you* – the rest of the world, the politicians – to say how the tools are used. The tools may be used for purposes which most of us would regard as bad. If so we are sorry. But as scientists, that is no concern of ours.

This is the doctrine of the ethical neutrality of science. I can't accept it for an instant. I don't believe any scientist of serious feeling can accept it. It is hard, some think, to find the precise statements which will prove it wrong. Yet we nearly all feel intuitively that the invention of comfortable categories is a moral trap. It is one of the easier methods of letting the conscience rust. It is exactly what the early nineteenth-century economists, such as Ricardo, did in the face of the facts of the first industrial revolution. We wonder now how men, intelligent men, can have been so morally blind. We realize how the exposure of that moral blindness gave Marxism its apocalyptic force. We are now, in the middle of the scientific or second industrial revolution, in something like the same position as Ricardo. Are we going to let our consciences rust? Can we ignore that intimation we nearly all have, that scientists have a unique responsibility? Can we believe it, that science is morally neutral?

To me – it would be dishonest to pretend otherwise – there is only one answer to those questions. Yet I have been brought up in the presence of the same intellectual categories as most Western scientists. It would be dishonest to pretend that I find it easy to construct a rationale which expresses what I now believe. The best I can hope for is to fire a few sighting shots. Perhaps someone who sees more clearly than I can will come along and make a real job of it.

Let me begin by a remark which seems some way off the point. Anyone who has ever worked in science knows how much aesthetic joy he has obtained. That is, in the actual *activity* of science, in the process of making a discovery, however humble it is, one can't help feeling an awareness of beauty. The subjective experience, the aesthetic satisfaction, seems exactly the same as the satisfaction one gets from writing a poem or a novel, or composing a piece of music. I don't think anyone has succeeded in distinguishing between them. The literature of scientific discovery is full of this aesthetic joy. The very best communication of it that I know comes in G. H. Hardy's book *A Mathematician's Apology*. Graham Greene once said he thought that, along with Henry James's prefaces, this was the best account of the artistic experience ever written. But one meets the same thing throughout the history of science. Bolyai's great yell of triumph when he saw he could construct a self-consistent non-Euclidian geometry: Rutherford's revelation to his colleagues that he knew what the atom was like: Darwin's slow, patient, timorous certainty that at last he had got there – all these are voices, different voices, of aesthetic ecstasy.

That is not the end of it. The *result* of the activity of science, the actual finished piece of scientific work, has an aesthetic value in itself. The judgements passed on it by other scientists will, more often than not, be expressed in aesthetic terms: 'That's beautiful,' or 'That really is very pretty!' (as the understating English tend to say). The aesthetics of scientific constructs, like the aesthetics of works of art, are variegated. We think some of the great syntheses, like Newton's, beautiful because of their classical simplicity, but we see a different kind of beauty in the relativistic extension of the wave equation, or the interpretation of the structure of dioxyribonucleic acid, perhaps because of the touch of unexpectedness. But scientists know their kinds of beauty when they see them. They are suspicious, and scientific history shows they have always been right to be so, when a subject is in an 'ugly' state. For example, most physicists feel in their bones that the present bizarre assembly of nuclear particles, as grotesque as a stamp collection, can't possibly be, in the long run, the last word.

We should not restrict the aesthetic values to what we call 'pure' science. Applied science has its beauties, which are, in my view, identical in nature. The magnetron has been a marvellously useful device, yet it was a beautiful device, not exactly apart from its utility, but because it did, with such supreme economy, precisely what it was designed to do. Right down in the field of development, the aesthetic experience is just as real to engineers. When they forget it, when they begin to design heavy power equipment about twice as heavy as it needs to be, engineers are the first to know that they are lacking virtue.

There is no doubt, then, about the aesthetic content of science, both in the activity and the result. But aesthetics has no connection with morals, say the categorizers. I don't want to waste time on peripheral issues – but are you quite sure of that? Or is it possible that these categories are inventions to make us evade the human and social conditions in which we now exist? But let's move straight on to something else, which is right in the grain of the activity of science and which is at the same time quintessentially moral. I mean, the desire to find the truth.

By *truth* I don't intend anything complicated, once again. I am using truth as a scientist uses it. We all know that the philosophical examination of the concept of empirical truth gets us into some curious complexities, but most scientists really don't care. They know that the truth, as they use the word, and as the rest of us use it in the language of human speech, is what makes science work. That is good enough for them. On it rests the whole great edifice of modern science. They have a sneaking sympathy for Rutherford who, when asked to examine the philosophical bases of science, was inclined to reply, as he did to the metaphysician, Samuel Alexander: 'Well, what have you been talking all your life, Alexander? Just hot air! Nothing but hot air!'

Anyway, truth in their own straightforward sense is what scientists are trying to find. They want to find what is *there*. Without that desire, there is no science. It is the driving-force of the whole activity. It compels the scientist to have an overriding respect for truth, every stretch of the way. That is, if you're going to find what is *there*, you must not deceive yourself or anyone else. You mustn't lie to yourself. At the crudest level, you mustn't fake your experiments.

Curiously enough, scientists do try to behave like that. A short time ago I wrote a novel where the story hinged on a case of scientific fraud. But I made one of my characters, who was himself a very good scientist, say that, considering the opportunities and temptations, it is astonishing how few such cases there are. We have all heard of perhaps half a dozen open and notorious ones, which are on the record for anyone to read – ranging from the 'discovery' of L-radiation to the singular episode of the Piltdown man.

We have all, if we have lived any time in the scientific world, heard private talk of something like another dozen cases which for various reasons are not yet public property. In some of those cases, we know the motives for cheating – sometimes, but not always, sheer personal advantage, such as getting money or a job. But not always. A special kind of vanity has led more than one man into scientific faking. At a lower level of research, there are presumably some more cases. There must have been occasional PhD students who scraped by with the help of a bit of fraud.

But the total number of all these men is vanishingly small by the side of the total number of scientists. Incidentally, the effect on science of such frauds is also vanishingly small. Science is a self-correcting system. That is, no fraud (or honest mistake) is going to stay undetected for long. There is no need for an extrinsic scientific criticism, because criticism is inherent in the process itself. So that all that a fraud can do is waste the time of the scientists who have to clear it up.

The remarkable thing is not the handful of scientists who deviate from the search for truth but the overwhelming numbers who keep to it. That is a demonstration, absolutely clear for anyone to see, of moral behaviour on a very large scale.

We take it for granted. Yet it is very important. It differentiates science in its widest sense (which includes scholarship) from all other intellectual activities. There is a built-in moral component right in the core of the scientific activity itself. The desire to find the truth is itself a moral impulse, or at least contains a moral impulse. The way in which a scientist tries to find the truth imposes on him a constant moral discipline. We say a scientific conclusion – such as the contradiction of parity by Lee and Yang – is 'true' in the limited sense of scientific truth, just as we say that it is 'beautiful' according to the criteria of scientific aesthetics. We also know that to reach this conclusion took a set of actions which would have been useless without the moral motive. That is, all through the experiments of Wu and her colleagues, there was the constant moral exercise of seeking and telling the truth. To scientists, who are brought up in this climate, this seems as natural as breathing. Yet it is a wonderful thing. Even if the scientific activity contained only this one moral component, that would be enough to let us say that it was morally un-neutral.

But is this the only moral component? All scientists would agree about the beauty and the truth. In the Western world, they wouldn't agree on much more. Some will feel with me in what I'm going to say. Some will not. That doesn't affect me much, except that I am worried by the growth of an attitude I think very dangerous, a kind of technological conformity disguised as cynicism. I shall say a little more about that later. As for disagreement, G. H. Hardy used to comment that a serious man never ought to waste his time stating a majority opinion – there are plenty of others to do that. That was the voice of classical scientific non-conformity. I wish that we heard it more often.

Let me cite some grounds for hope. Any of us who were doing science before 1933 can remember what the atmosphere was like. It is a terrible bore when ageing men speak about the charms of their youth. Yet I'm going to irritate you – just as Talleyrand irritated his juniors – by saying that unless one was on the scene before 1933, one hasn't known the sweetness of the scientific life. The scientific world of the Twenties was as near a full-fledged international community as we're likely to get. Don't think I'm saying that the men involved were superhuman or free from the ordinary frailties. That wouldn't come well from me, who've spent a fraction of my writing-life pointing out that scientists are, first and foremost, men. But the atmosphere of the Twenties in science was filled with an air of benevolence and magnanimity which transcended the people who lived in it.

Anyone who ever spent a week in Cambridge or Göttingen or Copenhagen felt it all round him. Rutherford had many human faults, but he was a great man with abounding human generosity. For him the world of science was a world that lived on a plane above the nation-state, and lived there with joy. That was at least as true of those two other great men, Niels Bohr and Franck, and some of that spirit rubbed off on to the pupils round them. The same was true of the Roman school of physics.

The personal links within this international world were very close. It is worth remembering that Peter Kapitsa, who was a loyal Soviet citizen, honoured my country by working in Rutherford's laboratory for many years. He became a Fellow of the Royal Society, a Fellow of Trinity College, Cambridge, and the founder and king pin of the best physics club Cambridge has known. He never gave up his Soviet citizenship and is now Director of the Institute of Physical Problems in Moscow. Through him a generation of English scientists came to have personal knowledge of Russian scientists. These exchanges were then, and have remained, more valuable than all the diplomatic exchanges ever invented.

The Kapitsa phenomenon couldn't take place now. I hope to live to see the day when a young Kapitsa can once more work for sixteen years in Berkeley or Cambridge and then go back to an eminent place in his own country. When that can happen, we are all right. But after the idyllic years of world science we passed into a tempest of history: and, I suppose by an unfortunate coincidence, we passed into a technological tempest too.

The discovery of atomic fission broke up the world of international physics. 'This has killed a beautiful subject,' said Mark Oliphant, the father-figure of Australian physics, in 1945, after the bombs had dropped. In intellectual terms, he has not turned out right. But in spiritual or moral terms, I sometimes think he has.

A good deal of the international community of science remains in other fields – in great areas of biology, for example. Many biologists are feeling the identical liberation, the identical joy at taking part in a magnanimous enterprise, that physicists felt in the Twenties. It is more than likely that the moral and intellectual leadership of science will pass to the biologists, and it is among them that we shall find the Einsteins, Rutherfords and Bohrs of the next generation.

Physicists have had a bitterer task. With the discovery of fission, and with some technical breakthroughs in electronics, physicists became, almost overnight, the most important military resource a nation-state could call on. A large number of physicists became soldiers-not-in-uniform. So they have remained, in the advanced societies, ever since.

It is very difficult to see what else they could have done. All this began in the Hitler war. Most scientists thought then that Nazism was as near absolute evil as a human society can manage. I myself think so, without qualification. That being so, Nazism had to be fought, and since the Nazis might make fission bombs –

which we thought possible until 1944 and which was a constant nightmare if one was remotely in the know – well, then, we had to make them too. Unless one was an unlimited pacifist, there was nothing else to do. And unlimited pacifism is a position which most of us cannot sustain.

Therefore I respect, and to a large extent share, the moral attitudes of those scientists who devoted themselves to making the bomb. But the trouble is, when you get on to any kind of moral escalator, to know whether you're ever going to be able to get off. When scientists become soldiers, they give up something, so imperceptibly that they don't realize it, of the full scientific life. Not intellectually. I see no evidence that scientific work on weapons of maximum destruction has been in any intellectual respect different from other scientific work. But there is a moral difference.

It may be – and scientists who are better men than I am often take this attitude, and I have tried to represent it faithfully in one of my books – that this is a moral price which, in certain circumstances, has to be paid. Nevertheless, it is no good pretending that there is not a moral price. Soldiers have to obey. That is the foundation of their morality. It is not the foundation of the scientific morality. Scientists have to question, and if necessary to rebel. I don't want to be misunderstood. I am no anarchist. I am not suggesting that loyalty is not a prime virtue. I am not saying that all rebellion is good. But I am saying that loyalty can easily turn into conformity, and that conformity can often be a cloak for the timid and self-seeking. So can obedience, carried to the limit. When you think of the long and gloomy history of man, you will find that far more, and more hideous, crimes have been committed in the name of obedience than have ever been committed in the name of rebellion. If you doubt that, read William Shirer's *Rise and Fall of the Third Reich*. The German officer corps were brought up in the most rigorous code of obedience. To themselves, no more honourable and God-fearing body of men could conceivably exist. Yet in the name of obedience they were party to, and assisted in, the most wicked large-scale actions in the history of the world.

Scientists must not go that way. Yet the duty to question is not much of a support when you're living in the middle of an organized society. I speak with feeling here. I was an official for twenty years. I went into official life at the beginning of the war, for the reasons that prompted my scientific friends to make weapons. I stayed in that life until a year ago, for the same reason that made my scientific friends turn into civilian soldiers. The official's life in England is not quite so disciplined as a soldier's, but it is very nearly so. I think I know the virtues, which are very great, of the men who live that disciplined life. I also know what for me was the moral trap. I, too, had got on to an escalator. I can put the result in a sentence: I was hiding behind the institution, I was losing the power to say 'No'.

Only a very bold man, when he is a member of an organized society, can keep the power to say 'No'. I tell you that, not being a very bold man or one who finds it congenial to stand alone, away from his colleagues. We can't expect many scientists to do it. Is there any tougher ground for them to stand on? I suggest to you that there is. I believe that there is a spring of moral action in the scientific activity which is at least as strong as the search for truth. The name of this spring is *Knowledge*. Scientists *know* certain things in a fashion more immediate and more certain than those who don't know what science is. Unless we are abnormally weak or abnormally wicked men, this knowledge is bound to shape our actions. Most of us are timid, but to an extent, knowledge gives us guts. Perhaps it can give us guts strong enough for the jobs in hand.

Let me take the most obvious example. All physical scientists *know* that it is astonishingly easy to make plutonium. We know this, not as a journalistic fact at second hand, but as a fact in our own experience. We can work out the number of scientific and engineering personnel it needs for a nation-state to equip itself with fission and fusion bombs. We *know* that for a dozen or more states, it would only take perhaps five years, perhaps less. Even the best informed of us always exaggerate these periods.

This we know, with the certainty of – what shall I call it – engineering truth. We also, most of us, are familiar with statistics and the nature of odds. We know, with the certainty of established truth, that if enough of these weapons are made, by enough different states, some of them are going to blow up – through accident, or folly, or madness; but the numbers don't matter, what does matter is the nature of the statistical fact.

All this we *know*. We know it in a more direct sense than any politician can know it, because it comes from our direct experience. It is part of our minds. Are we going to let it happen?

All this we *know*. It throws upon scientists a direct and formal responsibility. It is not enough to say scientists have a responsibility as citizens. They have a much greater one than that, and one different in kind. For scientists have a moral imperative to say what they know. It is going to make them unpopular in their own nation-states. It may do worse than make them unpopular. That doesn't matter. Or at least, it does matter to you and me, but it must not count in the face of the risks.

For we genuinely know the risks. We are faced with an either/or and we haven't much time. The *either* is acceptance of a restriction of nuclear armaments. This is going to begin, just as a token, with an agreement on the stopping of nuclear tests. The United States is not going to get the 99.9 per cent 'security' that it has been asking for. This is unobtainable, though there are other bargains that the United States could probably secure. I am not going to conceal from you that this course involves certain risks. They are quite obvious, and no honest man is going to blink them. That is the *either*. The *or* is not a risk but a certainty. It is this. There is no agreement on tests. The nuclear arms race between the United

States and the USSR not only continues but accelerates. Other countries join in. Within, at the most, six years, China and six other states have a stock of nuclear bombs. Within, at the most, ten years, some of those bombs are going off. I am saying this as responsibly as I can. *That* is the certainty. On the one side, therefore, we have a finite risk. On the other side, we have a certainty of disaster. Between a wish and a certainty, a sane man does not hesitate.

It is the plain duty of scientists to explain the either/or. It is a duty which seems to me to live in the moral nature of the scientific activity itself.

The same duty, though in a much more pleasant form, arises with respect to the benevolent powers of science. For scientists know, and again with the certainty of scientific knowledge, that we possess every scientific fact we need to transform the physical life of half the world. And transform within the span of people now living. I mean, we have all the resources to help half the world live as long as we do, and eat enough. All that is missing is the will. We *know* that. Just as we know that you in the United States, and to a slightly less extent, we in the United Kingdom, have been almost unimaginably lucky. We are sitting like people in a smart and cosy restaurant, and we are eating comfortably, looking out of the window into the streets. Down on the pavement are people looking up at us, people who by chance have different coloured skins from ours, and are rather hungry. Do you wonder that they don't like us all that much? Do you wonder that we sometimes feel ashamed of ourselves as we look out through the plate glass?

Well, it is within our power to get started on that problem. We are morally impelled to. We all know that, if the human species does solve that one, there will be consequences which are themselves problems. For instance, the population of the world will become embarrassingly large. But that is another challenge. There are going to be challenges to our intelligence and to our moral nature as long as man remains man. After all, a challenge is not, as the word is coming to be used, an excuse for slinking off and doing nothing. A challenge is something to be picked up.

For all those reasons, I believe the world community of scientists has a final responsibility upon it – a greater responsibility than is pressing on any other body of men. I do not pretend to know how they will bear this responsibility. These may be famous last words, but I have an inextinguishable hope. For, as I have said tonight, there is no doubt that the scientific activity is both beautiful and truthful. I cannot prove it, but I believe that, simply because scientists cannot escape their own knowledge, they won't be able to avoid showing themselves disposed to good.

Index

Note: numbers in italics refer to diagrams, illustrations and captions

Acknowledgements

The publishers and the Executors of the Estate of Lord Snow would like to thank Nigel Henbest for his invaluable assistance as scientific adviser. Einstein's letter to President Roosevelt is reproduced by kind permission of the Estate of Albert Einstein. 'The moral un-neutrality of science' first appeared in *Public Affairs*, published by Macmillan in 1971.

The publishers wish to thank the following for permission to reproduce photographs and illustrations:

Argonne National Laboratory, pages 78 and 82;
Graham Ashton, page 121;
Associated Press, pages 141 *above left* and *above right*, 155 *above left* and *below left*;
BBC Hulton Picture Library, pages 28, 36, 47, 87, 114, 136 and 165;
The Bettman Archive, pages 19, 23, 24, 49, 69 and 95;
Niels Bohr Institute, page 66;
Paul Brierly, pages 151, 155 *right*, 158 *above* and 161;
Camera Press, pages 81, 141 *below left* and *below right*, 167 and 172/173;
Cavendish Laboratory, Cambridge, pages 38, 40/41, 65 and 86;
Chicago Historical Society, pages 108/109;
Colorific, page 125 *below*;

John Hillelson Agency, pages 45 (photo Erich Lessing), 147 (photo Armel Brucelle, Sygma) and 162 (photo Leonard Freed);
Illustrated London News, page 97 *below*;
Imperial War Museum, pages 101, 119 *below* and 169 *above*;
Los Alamos Scientific Laboratory, page 118;
Marconi Company Ltd, page 158 *below*;
National Portrait Gallery, London, pages 20 and 33;
The New Scientist, London, page 148 (photo Eric Gemmell);
Nordisk Pressefoto, pages 58 and 64;
Politikens Pressefoto, pages 51 and 59;
Popperfoto, pages 34, 61, 77, 98 *above* and *below*, 119 *above*, 124, 125 *above*, 126/127, 129, 132 *left*, 138/139, 155 *centre* and 168/169;
Rex Features, page 132 *right*;
Salford Art Gallery, page 163;
Science Photo Library, pages 15, 135, 144, 145, 146 and 175;
Ullstein Bilderdienst, pages 27, 43, 90 and 93 *above* and *below*;
University of California, Bancroft Library, page 99;
University of Chicago, page 111 *above* and *below*;
University of Texas at Austin, Humanities Research Centre, pages 30/31, 44 and 53.